Ten Steps Toward Christ is a book to read
Jimmy Evans' down-to-earth explanation
of faith will encourage, challenge, and cha. ~ ~ ~ ~... ....side out.

CRAIG GROESCHEL
Senior Pastor of Life.Church
Author of *WEIRD, Because Normal Isn't Working*

Pastor Jimmy Evans was instrumental in my own spiritual formation, and I truly believe this book will serve to build and strengthen you as well. Take the challenge to go deeper as you journey through this rich revelation of the Holy Spirit, Christ, and the God we call Father.

BRADY BOYD
Senior Pastor of New Life Church
Author of *Fear No Evil*

Nearly 20 years ago in a small prayer gathering, Jimmy Evans told me how God had called him to strengthen marriages and families. I have observed with amazement the supernatural effectiveness God has bestowed upon him. In this book, Jimmy shares practical information on developing a victorious life in Christ. Clearly, a journey to the heart of God will have a positive impact on our relationships with one another. I have witnessed how the truths shared in this book have totally transformed lives.

JAMES ROBISON
President of LIFE Outreach International

If you've never read a book by Jimmy Evans, you're about to find out why so many of us are huge fans of his resources. It's his honesty, pure and simple. As you journey with him on these *Ten Steps Toward Christ*, you will relate to his struggles and share in his victories. In the end, you'll come away with a more vibrant, victorious life in Christ.

CHRIS HODGES
Senior Pastor of Church of the Highlands

JIMMY EVANS

TEN STEPS TOWARD CHRIST

JOURNEY TO THE HEART OF GOD

Ten Steps Toward Christ: Journey to the Heart of God
Copyright © 2018 by Jimmy Evans

Ten Steps Toward Christ was originally published by Trinity Fellowship
Church in 2011.

Scripture taken from the New King James Version®. Copyright © 1982 by
Thomas Nelson. Used by permission. All rights reserved.

ISBN: 978-1-960870-00-1 (Paperback)
ISBN: 978-1-950113-97-2 (eBook)

XO Publishing® has no responsibility for the persistence or accuracy of URLs
for external or third-party Internet websites referred to in this publication and
does not guarantee that any content on such websites is, or will remain,
accurate or appropriate.

For more information, address XO Marriage®
1021 Grace Lane
Southlake, Texas 76092
1-800-360-6330
For more information, please visit XOMarriage.com.

Printed in the United States of America

23 24 25 26—5 4 3 2

To my precious granddaughter, Kate Sophia Evans.
You are a special girl and bring so much joy
to Lollie and Pappy.

Contents

Acknowledgments

A project of this size takes a team to pull it off. It has been my pleasure to work alongside an excellent group of people that have made this book possible. Matt Spears has led the team that worked on every aspect of this book.

To my son, Brent Evans: Thank you for walking beside me in this mission to share God's Good News with so many people. I love you and am so proud of you.

Of course, I always have my beautiful wife, Karen, to thank for her unending prayers, encouragement, and support. She is my biggest cheerleader. Karen, I love you and appreciate you more than I can say.

Most of all, I want to thank You, Jesus, for saving me and patiently loving me since May 1973 when I was born again into Your kingdom. Lord Jesus, You are my Rock. You have led me every step of the journey I will be explaining in this book. You alone deserve all glory and praise!

Introduction

I was born in 1953 and regularly attended church while I was growing up. I always considered myself to be a Christian, and I would have been offended if anyone had said otherwise. Like most people, I considered myself to be a "good person." And don't good people go to heaven?

In spite of my church attendance and pride in how "good" I was, I became increasingly immoral and rebellious. By the time I graduated from high school and went to college, I was completely absorbed in living to please myself and gratifying every desire I had, regardless of what anyone else thought about it.

I took a copy of the New Testament called *Good News for Modern Man* to college with me and kept it on the nightstand beside my bed. I am ashamed to say that just about the only time I read it was when I was drunk. I would come home after a night with my friends, and before I passed out, I would read a page or two of the New Testament. I didn't understand much of it, but I liked Jesus. I thought He was a really good person.

One of the best things that ever happened to me was meeting my wife, Karen. We met in biology class when we were sophomores in high school. Our dating experience was pretty rocky because of my lifestyle, but I really loved her, and we dated throughout high school.

Karen invited Christ into her heart around the time we met. She attended a weekly Bible study and was growing in her faith as we dated. I liked how pure she was, but I didn't share her zeal for the Lord—quite the opposite, in fact. As she grew in her faith, I became worse.

During my second year in college, Karen and I became engaged and set a date to be married. I wanted to marry her, but I had no intention of giving up my ungodly friends or unrighteous behavior. At that point, Karen didn't know how immoral I had become and didn't know about all the things I did with my friends, such as drinking, viewing pornography, and using profanity.

Karen appealed to me many times to become more interested in the Lord and to go to church with her. I never completely rejected her pleas, but I did everything possible to avoid what she was asking. As the time grew closer for us to get married, Karen talked with me more often about my relationship with my ungodly friends and my need for the Lord. I defended my friends and, just to pacify her, told her what I thought she wanted to hear about Jesus.

One week before our wedding, my friends threw a bachelor party for me. I was excited about it. Being the "good person" that I was, though, I told my friends that I only wanted to get drunk and play poker; I didn't want to be immoral that night. And on the night of the party, that's how it started out. We got drunk and played poker. Everything was going just as I had planned ... except for one thing. As soon as I was drunk, my friends brought in some girls they had invited without my knowledge. Within the hour, I had cheated on Karen. I don't remember a lot about that night because of how drunk I was, but I do remember that.

When I woke up the next morning, I stumbled into the bathroom with my usual hangover. What happened next changed my life forever. I looked at myself in the mirror as I washed my face, something I had done many times before. But this time, something was different. For the first time I didn't like the person I was looking at.

I had been drunk and immoral many nights before and had never felt bad about it. Even though I typically felt empty and somewhat disappointed after my nights of sin, I never felt guilty or sensed that I had done something wrong. But as I said, this time was different.

As I looked in the mirror that morning, I knew I had sinned against God and against Karen. I stood there feeling confused and guilty, hearing the words of our preacher ringing in my ears. He would say, "If Jesus isn't Lord of all, He isn't Lord at all." He would also say, "Being in church doesn't make you a Christian any more than standing in a garage makes you a car. You must be saved and receive Jesus as your Lord and Savior."

I had never paid much attention in church. I only went because I had to and because there were pretty girls at our church. But I am thankful that on that morning in the bathroom, I could remember a few things the preacher had said. Standing in front of the sink, looking at myself in the mirror, I realized I didn't want to live as I had been any longer.

I had lied to Karen and deceived her for years about who I really was. That had to come to an end. Even though I knew I could keep my sin the night before a secret and marry her as though nothing had happened, I decided to tell her.

Even more important than that decision was my decision to make Jesus the Lord of my life. As I stood in the bathroom, I spoke words to the Lord that changed me forever: "Lord Jesus, I am so sorry for my sin and rebellion. Today I make You the Lord of my life and surrender everything to You. I will live the rest of my life for You and not turn back. This isn't about Karen. I know she may not marry me because of what I have done. Regardless, I will follow You from now on. Please forgive me of my sins and come into my heart and be my Lord and Savior."

I was 19 years old when I prayed that prayer. Now, more than 40 years later, I can tell you that it was the best day of my life, and Jesus has been the best thing that has ever happened to me. He is *real*, and from the instant I prayed that prayer, I could sense something different inside me. It was Jesus filling my heart and coming into my life.

Going to church or being a "good person" doesn't make you a Christian. Being raised by Christian parents or having Christian friends doesn't make you a Christian either. You must make a personal decision to open your heart to Christ and invite Him to be your Lord and Savior. It is the most important decision you will ever make, and it won't just change your life—it will change your eternity.

By the way, after my experience in the bathroom that morning, I went over to Karen's house and told her what I had done. She was devastated and told me she wouldn't marry me. I was heartbroken. But I kept my commitment to the Lord.

Later that day I also broke off my relationship with my friends. I lost every friend I had that day and never again had anything to do with any of them. It was a crucial decision in my new Christian life.

A couple of days later, Karen began hearing from her friends what I had done. She called me to talk, and she could tell I had changed. We reconciled and were married on May 11, 1973.

Since that time, we have followed Christ, and He has blessed us greatly. I always thought being a dedicated Christian would be a boring, difficult life. Not true! Having lived in rebellion and sin, I can tell you that it is an empty and painful way to live. But living for Jesus Christ is the opposite. I love it! It is the most fulfilling and exciting way to live.

In 1982 I entered full-time ministry and have been a pastor ever since. The remainder of this book will chronicle what I have learned, experienced, and taught others as essential foundations in living for Christ. But this book isn't really about me. In fact, it's about you. It's about how you can draw nearer to God. I tell my story simply to illustrate truths every Christian needs to learn.

So if you're looking for a real and intimate relationship with Jesus and a fulfilling and blessed life, this book is for you. It provides an overview of 10 crucial steps that will lead you into a deeper relationship with Christ and a victorious experience as a believer.

You will notice many Scripture references throughout the book. This is for two reasons. First, it is to make the book as brief as possible by giving you the essential information and not going into too much detail. Second, and more importantly, it is to encourage you to read the Bible and learn to study it on your own. Every time you see a Scripture reference, look it up. This will help you to learn the Bible.

If you don't have a Bible, get one. Be sure and choose one that you can understand. I use the New King James Version because it is theologically sound as well as understandable. But there are other good translations to choose from as well. Your local Christian bookstore can help you make a good selection. Your Bible will become one of your most important possessions and an essential part of your life in Christ. May God richly bless you as you journey toward His heart.

JIMMY EVANS

TEN STEPS TOWARD CHRIST

JOURNEY TO THE HEART OF GOD

1

Being Born Again

There was a man of the Pharisees named Nicodemus, a ruler of the Jews. This man came to Jesus by night and said to Him, "Rabbi, we know that You are a teacher come from God; for no one can do these signs that You do unless God is with him."

Jesus answered and said to him, "Most assuredly, I say to you, unless one is born again, he cannot see the kingdom of God."

Nicodemus said to Him, "How can a man be born when he is old? Can he enter a second time into his mother's womb and be born?"

Jesus answered, "Most assuredly, I say to you, unless one is born of water and the Spirit, he cannot enter the kingdom of God. That which is born of the flesh is flesh, and that which is born of the Spirit is spirit. Do not marvel that I said to you, 'You must be born again.' The wind blows where it wishes, and you hear the sound of it, but cannot tell where it comes from and where it goes. So is everyone who is born of the Spirit."

Nicodemus answered and said to Him, "How can these things be?"

—John 3:1–9

Before I received Christ, I would hear people talking about being "born again." It sounded spooky and too spiritual for me. Yet even though I didn't understand it, I experienced it when I surrendered my life to Jesus. I was born "of the Spirit" on that day as I came alive to Christ and received the gift of eternal life (Romans 6:23).

To understand being born again, we need to take a quick trip back to the Garden of Eden and God's creation of Adam and Eve.

The Origin of Death

When God created Adam and Eve, He breathed life into their nostrils, and they became "living beings," (see Genesis 2:7). The breath God breathed into them wasn't just air; it was His Spirit breathing life into their spirits. Thus, they were alive as triune beings—body, soul, and spirit. However, God warned them not to eat of the fruit of the tree of the knowledge of good and evil. He warned them that on the day they ate of it they would die (Genesis 2:17).

Of course, Genesis 3 records how Satan, in the form of a serpent, tempted Adam and Eve and how they ate the forbidden fruit. At the moment they ate it, their bodies and souls didn't die, but their spirits did. The Spirit of God departed from them, and they became spiritually dead. They could no longer commune with God intimately, as they had done when He walked with them in the garden.

They were now incapable of spiritual life or relationship and were spiritually separated from God. As a result, their minds became darkened, their emotions corrupted, their relationship divided, and their bodies aged and decayed. They passed their fallen nature on to their children and the generations after them until the entire human race became utterly evil (Genesis 6:5–6). To this day, spiritual death and the natural tendency to rebel against God are inherent in all of us as a result of the fall of Adam and Eve (Romans 7:14–21).

The Gift of Spiritual Life

Jesus came to save us by dying for us on the cross and paying for our sins. It is a debt we can never pay. But because of Jesus' perfect life, God accepted His death as the payment for the sins of mankind. As we read in the Gospel of John:

> "For God so loved the world that He gave His only begotten Son, that whoever believes in Him should not perish but have everlasting life. For God did not send His Son into the world to condemn the world, but that the world through Him might be saved.
>
> He who believes in Him is not condemned; but he who does not believe is condemned already, because he has not believed in the name of the only begotten Son of God" (John 3:16–18).

By believing that Jesus is God's only Son sent into the world to pay for our sins, we are saved from sin and hell and born again of the Holy Spirit. This must include a recognition of the Lordship of Jesus and the fact that He alone is the Savior of the world.

Consider this passage from Romans, talking about the meaning of certain verses in the Old Testament:

> What does it say? "The word is near you, in your mouth and in your heart" (that is, the word of faith which we preach): that if you confess with your mouth the Lord Jesus and believe in your heart that God has raised Him from the dead, you will be saved. For with the heart one believes unto righteousness, and with the mouth confession is made unto salvation. For the Scripture says, "Whoever believes on Him will not be put to shame" (Romans 10:8–11).

This text makes it clear that we must confess with our mouths Jesus as Lord and believe that He was raised from the dead. These are two crucial issues to understand in becoming a true believer in Christ. First, without acknowledging the Lordship of Christ, we are simply buying "fire insurance" to save us from hell and make us feel better. A profession of faith that doesn't acknowledge Christ as Lord doesn't change the fundamental problem between God and us—rebellion (Matthew 7:22–23). Also, believing that God raised Jesus from the dead is essential because it signifies that only Jesus, and no other so-called savior, guru, or religious leader, satisfied the requirements of God to save us from our sins. The resurrection was God's public and eternal validation that Jesus was who He said He was and that His sacrifice for our sins was accepted.

Salvation occurs as we believe and confess in accordance with God's will. That is all we have to do. Jesus did the hard part for us that we never could have done. Now, by believing and confessing, we can freely receive salvation from God.

There is nothing we can do to deserve it. We can only accept it or reject it.

Here is the way the apostle Paul describes salvation as a free gift:

> And you *He made alive,* who were dead in trespasses and sins, in which you once walked according to the course of this world, according to the prince of the power of the air, the spirit who now works in the sons of disobedience, among whom also we all once conducted ourselves in the lusts of our flesh, fulfilling the desires of the flesh and of the mind, and were by nature children of wrath, just as the others.
>
> But God, who is rich in mercy, because of His great love with which He loved us, even when we were dead in trespasses, made us alive together with Christ (by grace you have been saved), and raised *us* up together, and made *us* sit together in the heavenly *places* in Christ Jesus, that in the ages to come He might show the exceeding riches of His grace in *His* kindness toward us in Christ Jesus. For by grace you have been saved through faith, and that not of yourselves; *it is* the gift of God, not of works, lest anyone should boast (Ephesians 2:1–9).

Through faith in God's Word, we believe that our sins have been paid for by Jesus on the cross, as was attested by His resurrection from the dead (Isaiah 53:3–5; Romans 1:3–4; Galatians 3:13–14). Also, by faith, we confess Jesus as the Lord of our lives (Romans 10:9). The title *Lord* means "master" or "boss." Using (and meaning) it means we are stepping down from the throne of our lives and asking Jesus to fill the throne that was designed for Him from the beginning.

Being saved and born again doesn't just mean that we now believe something we didn't believe before. That is simply a mental exercise which, on its own, provides no benefits. What you think doesn't make you a Christian. Being born again takes place as you make a radical decision to change the purpose of your life. No longer are you living for self and sin; now you are ready to surrender your life to Christ and follow Him as your Lord.

As we repent of our sins and rebellion against God and as we confess Jesus as our Lord and invite Him into our hearts, He comes in and forgives all our sins and gives us the gift of eternal life (Revelation 3:20). We are now capable of spiritual relationship and communion with God.

This isn't some dead religion. It is a dynamic, personal relationship with God.

Your Opportunity

Over 40 years ago, as a confused and rebellious young man, I prayed a prayer to confess my sins and invite Christ into my heart. It radically changed my life, and the salvation it brought is just as real today as it was then. That was not only the most important thing I have ever done in my life; it was also the most important thing I will ever do in all eternity.

The day you receive Christ and become born again is your spiritual birthday and the most important day in your life. Are you ready to make Jesus your Lord? If so, pray this prayer:

Lord Jesus, I have sinned and rebelled against You, a holy God. There is no excuse, and I confess my sins to You now and repent of my rebellion. I ask for Your forgiveness. I believe that You died on the cross for my sins. I receive Your forgiveness now and believe that Your blood is more powerful than my worst sins. I am now totally forgiven by You, and I forgive myself. The past is behind me. I confess You now as my Lord and Savior. I step down from the throne of my heart, and I pray that You will now sit on that throne as my Lord and King. Come into my heart and give me the gift of eternal life. I know I don't deserve it, but I receive it by faith as a gift of grace. I believe I am now forgiven, born again, and on my way to heaven. I will live the rest of my life for You. Fill me with Your Holy Spirit and lead me, speak to me, and give me the power to change, make right decisions, and live for You. In Jesus' name, Amen.

If you sincerely prayed that prayer, then congratulations! You are born again. You are eternally changed, and your salvation is secure in Christ. Your name has been written in the book of life in heaven (Philippians 4:3; Revelation 21:27). You may feel strong feelings or no feelings—it doesn't matter. God isn't dependent upon your feelings. He is faithful to do what He has promised, and you must live by faith, not feelings.

But let me give you a warning: Once you have prayed that prayer and begun your new life in Christ, the devil will probably whisper into your heart that it isn't real. He'll tell you things like "God loves others, but you are too bad to be saved." That is what he said to me when I got saved. He was trying to discourage me. I didn't know how to discern the devil's voice then, but I do now. So take my advice. Every time you hear a voice inside your mind or heart that is trying to discourage you, condemn you, or keep you from getting closer to God or doing God's will, it is of the devil. Refuse to acknowledge it and continue on your course.

Now that you are a new Christian, it is important to tell other believers about the decision you've made. Chapter 4 of this book will tell you about the importance of Christian relationships in our lives. I would never have made it as a new believer unless I had made the decision (which I did) to walk away from some old friends and to begin new relationships with fellow believers. I encourage you to tell a pastor, church leader, believing family member, or a Christian friend about the decision you've made to live for Christ. Also, get involved in a Bible-believing church. It is the best environment possible to meet the right friends and to grow spiritually.

At the back of this book, I have included a spiritual birth certificate for you to record this important day if you prayed the prayer to receive Christ. Tear it out, fill it in, and keep it in your Bible or some other safe place. As time goes on, it will become even more special to you. It will also become a physical testimony to the spiritual fact that you are now born again.

You've taken step one. Now for the next step!

2

Covenants of Water Baptism and Communion

And Jesus came and spoke to them, saying, "All authority has been given to Me in heaven and on earth. Go therefore and make disciples of all the nations, baptizing them in the name of the Father and of the Son and of the Holy Spirit, teaching them to observe all things that I have commanded you; and lo, I am with you always, *even* to the end of the age." Amen.

—Matthew 28:18–20

"He who believes and is baptized shall be saved."

—Mark 16:16

The Scriptures above are Jesus commanding believers to be baptized by water once they are saved. The New Testament word for *baptize* means to "immerse." Therefore, water baptism means to be immersed under water. Most evangelical churches have a baptistry where new believers are water-baptized. But I know of many people who are baptized in swimming pools, lakes, rivers, bathtubs, and so on.

When I received Christ, I was a Baptist, and needless to say—they baptized me! I'm thankful for the fact that they led me into that step of obedience. Even though I didn't under-stand the full significance of it at the time, I now realize how critically important it was as a step toward a successful relationship with Christ.

I have noticed that many people have questions about baptism. One of the most common questions is "Why is baptism so important?" Another is "If I don't get water-bap-tized, can I still be saved?"

I want to answer those questions as I begin to explain the meaning of water baptism. And then we'll get to another vital act of obedience for all Christians. As we'll discover, both are part of our covenant with God through Christ.

Two Big Questions

Let me begin by addressing the importance of water baptism. I hope you will see that water baptism is, in fact, a crucial next step after receiving Christ as your Lord and Savior.

Why is getting baptized so important?

If for no other reason, baptism is important because Jesus commanded it and even had it done to Himself as an act of obedience to God the Father (Matthew 3:13–16). And Jesus is to be obeyed because He is Lord. Remember, the title *Lord* means "boss." If we won't do the first thing Jesus tells us to do once we are saved, that's not a good sign—it reveals insin-cerity in our faith. We must get used to doing things that we don't completely understand and aren't comfortable with if we are going to be faithful followers of Christ.

Now, I know of many people who will acknowledge Jesus intellectually but won't follow through with water baptism because of embarrassment or the possibility of being rejected or even persecuted by others. In short, they fear social consequences. But this is one of the reasons why Jesus commanded us to be baptized.

He hung naked on a cross at the crossroads of the world, in front of His mother and close friends, as He was mocked and humiliated for our sake. At Calvary, Jesus wasn't ashamed of being identified with us and paying for the sins we would commit. We must ask ourselves an important question: Are we ashamed of Jesus? That question begs another one: Are we going to be public Christians or private ones? And still another: Are we going to care more about what Jesus thinks or what other people think?

I can tell you right now—if you care more about being admired and accepted by people than you care about pleasing God, you will be a poor follower of Christ, and your life will never make much of a difference.

Listen to what Jesus says to some of His followers about this issue:

> "Whoever confesses Me before men, him I will also confess before My Father who is in heaven. But whoever denies Me before men, him I will also deny before My Father who is in heaven" (Matthew 10:32–33).

The context of Jesus' statement is the fear of man and how some people refused to publicly identify with Him because of what others might think about them or do to them. Jesus' statement is simple: if we are ashamed of Him in front of people, He will be ashamed of us as our representative before God the Father.

I can tell you that whatever bad things people might do to you as a Christian, they pale in comparison with how much God will bless you for obedience. Always choose God. You will never regret it. This applies to obedience in water baptism as well as so many other things.

Can I be saved if I don't get water-baptized?

The short answer is yes. But it is a qualified yes. Let me explain.

The thief on the cross next to Jesus recognized Him as Lord and King, and as a result, Jesus said they would be together in Paradise that very day (Luke 23:39–43). Of course, the thief couldn't be baptized. It was a physical impossibility. But he still got to heaven!

Likewise, there are people who receive Christ on their deathbeds, on a crashing plane, or through other circumstances in which being water-baptized isn't practical or even possible. And there are others who receive Christ but are never taught about water baptism.

I also know of many people who were baptized (sprinkled) as children and were taught that their infant baptism is all that is necessary. However, this is not true.

Your parents may mean well, but no one can make the decision for you to be saved or baptized but you. Being sprinkled or baptized as an infant may be a genuine token of parents dedicating their child to God and themselves as godly parents, but that is all it is. We must make the decision to receive Christ ourselves, and the act of water baptism is meaningful only after we have made our own personal commitment.

So, to summarize: we can be saved without being baptized as long as there are circumstances that justify it. God is a gracious and reasonable God. However, if we know about the commandment to be water-baptized but refuse to obey, it raises questions about our sincerity in making Christ the Lord of our lives.

What Water Baptism Means

Being water-baptized means we are publicly identifying ourselves with Christ as His followers. It means we are declaring our love and loyalty to Him. It is a public act that signifies two private decisions we've made.

The first private decision is to die to sin and live for Christ. The apostle Paul speaks about this:

> In Him you were also circumcised with the circumcision made without hands, by putting off the body of the sins of the flesh, by the circumcision of Christ, buried with Him in baptism, in which you also were raised with *Him* through faith in the working of God, who raised Him from the dead (Colossians 2:11–12).

In other words, when we go into the baptism waters, it symbolizes death to sin and self and being raised up a new person to live for God. It signifies that we have truly been born again as a new creation in Christ (2 Corinthians 5:17).

The second private decision is to receive Christ's death as the payment for our sins and failures. As the apostle Peter says,

> There is also an antitype which now saves us—baptism
> (not the removal of the filth of the flesh, but the answer
> of a good conscience toward God), through the resurrec-
> tion of Jesus Christ, who has gone into heaven and is at
> the right hand of God, angels and authorities and powers
> having been made subject to Him (1 Peter 3:21–22).

Peter reveals to us here that water baptism doesn't mean that we are only washed from our sins on a physical, earthly level. After His resurrection, Jesus went into the temple in heaven and poured His blood upon the mercy seat to pay for our sins once and for all. By faith in Jesus' finished work on the cross, our consciences have now been purified so we can be free from our past and enjoy an intimate relationship with God.

This is the very point made by the author of Hebrews:

> Christ came *as* High Priest of the good things to come,
> with the greater and more perfect tabernacle not made
> with hands, that is, not of this creation. Not with the
> blood of goats and calves, but with His own blood He
> entered the Most Holy Place once for all, having obtained
> eternal redemption. For if the blood of bulls and goats
> and the ashes of a heifer, sprinkling the unclean, sancti-
> fies for the purifying of the flesh, how much more shall
> the blood of Christ, who through the eternal Spirit
> offered Himself without spot to God, cleanse your
> conscience from dead works to serve the living God?
> (Hebrews 9:11–14).

Water baptism is an important act that symbolizes powerful spiritual truths. Something supernatural happens in the baptismal waters. God meets us there and does something in our hearts that only He can do and that He does only through baptism.

Let me say it another way: I have never known a person who refused water baptism to have a strong relationship with Christ or do anything significant for the Lord. Bypassing baptism, whether on purpose or by accident, stunts our spiritual growth and impairs our ability to know God intimately.

Baptism: A Covenant of Commitment

Water baptism is a powerful and important step in stating publicly that we belong to Jesus and are committed to Him. In response, God blesses us and reveals Himself to us in a greater manner. Because we are not ashamed of Him, neither is He ashamed of us. Even though there are those who might claim to be sincere believers without being willing to be baptized in water, I doubt their commitment.

When I told Karen that I loved her and wanted to spend the rest of my life with her, I was willing to signify that commitment by standing in a public place and declaring my love and loyalty to her on our wedding day. Because of that, she didn't doubt the sincerity of my love or commitment. But the Lord knows how many men have sworn their unfailing love to a woman but refused to marry her and truly commit. It just isn't the same. Ask any woman!

Likewise, when I told Jesus that I loved Him and wanted to live my life for Him, He wanted a public ceremony— water baptism. I obeyed. Therefore, my conscience is clear before God as it relates to my commitment to Him and my obedience to His Lordship.

Water baptism is the covenant seal of our relationship with Christ. It consummates our formal commitment to Him with a tangible outward action, just as a wedding ceremony does between a man and woman as they enter into the covenant of marriage.

A covenant relationship is the most special and sacred relationship we can have. The word covenant means "to cut," and it conveys the meaning of a permanent, sacrificial relationship. Jesus established the new covenant with His own blood—He was cut (Luke 22:20). Through His sacrifice, He made a covenant with us to establish a permanent bond between us.

Our covenant with God is the most secure relationship we will ever have. But it has to be real. That is why God established water baptism as a tangible demonstration of what has happened between us. When God makes a covenant, there is always an outward sign as an unforgettable reminder of the special relationship that has been entered into.

The apostle Paul compares water baptism to the act of circumcision that God established as the seal and sign of the covenant He made with Abraham and his descendants (Colossians 2:11–14). Just as any Jewish male knew beyond a doubt that he was walking in covenant with God through physical circumcision, so we can have the same confidence through water baptism.

Paul calls baptism "the circumcision of Christ." He explains that it is no longer an outward circumcision (cutting away of physical flesh); it is the inward circumcision of our hearts to prepare us to live for God. According to Paul, it occurs as we are obedient through baptism. As you can see, water baptism is a big deal with serious spiritual symbolism and important meaning for the relationship between us and God.

Without being water-baptized, you may be a Christian (only God knows for sure), but I don't believe you can have the same confidence about that as others who have obeyed by being baptized. Also, since you won't take the first step Jesus commanded for you to take as a new believer, you will probably find reasons not to do other things that God will command you to do.

Be water-baptized! If you don't have a church, find a Bible-believing church and become a part of it. Tell the pastor or someone else in leadership there about your commitment to Christ. Ask the church to baptize you. If they don't baptize, it isn't a Bible-believing church—keep looking. If you are already part of a good church, tell them what you have done and be water-baptized. Don't put it off. You will never regret it, and you will find that it takes you to another level in your relationship with the Lord.

Still fearful about taking this step? Let me tell you: the devil will always try to use fear to keep you from doing what God wants you to do. I have had to face my fears hundreds of times as a believer. Fear is never from God (2 Timothy 1:7). It is from the devil, who tries to intimidate us as we seek to obey and serve God. Make up your mind right now that you will not be controlled by fear. You are going to be a person of faith! Take every step of obedience by faith and believe the promises of God.

Communion: A Covenant of Relationship

I want to tell you about another important tradition of the
Christian faith that, like water baptism, is a sacred sign of our
covenant relationship with Christ. Communion—or the Lord's
Supper, as it is also called—is the ongoing covenant sign of our
relationship with Christ. Jesus first instituted this act with
His disciples just before His crucifixion, and He commanded
us to do this in remembrance of Him (Luke 22:19–20). Here
is an account of the purpose and significance of communion
given by the apostle Paul:

> For I received from the Lord that which I also delivered
> to you: that the Lord Jesus on the *same* night in which He
> was betrayed took bread; and when He had given thanks,
> He broke *it* and said, "Take, eat; this is My body which is
> broken for you; do this in remembrance of Me." In the
> same manner *He* also *took* the cup after supper, saying,
> "This cup is the new covenant in My blood. This do, as
> often as you drink *it,* in remembrance of Me."
>
> For as often as you eat this bread and drink this cup,
> you proclaim the Lord's death till He comes.
>
> Therefore whoever eats this bread or drinks *this* cup of
> the Lord in an unworthy manner will be guilty of the body
> and blood of the Lord. But let a man examine himself,
> and so let him eat of the bread and drink of the cup. For
> he who eats and drinks in an unworthy manner eats and
> drinks judgment to himself, not discerning the Lord's
> body. For this reason many *are* weak and sick among
> you, and many sleep. For if we would judge ourselves, we
> would not be judged. But when we are judged, we are

chastened by the Lord, that we may not be condemned
with the world (1 Corinthians 11:23–32).

In this passage, Paul shares revelation that he received
directly from the Lord Himself. He begins by explaining that
every time we take the bread and the cup representing the body
and blood of Christ, we are proclaiming the Lord's death. In
other words, we are celebrating the fullness and freedom Jesus
gained for us through His substitutionary death on the cross.

Communion keeps us from forgetting about the most
important element of our faith—the love that Jesus revealed
for us on the cross. Through His loving act of taking our
place on the cross, the curse of sin was removed from our
lives as it was placed upon His own body (Galatians 3:13–14).
Jesus' blood was shed to remove our sins so we could have an
eternal and intimate relationship with God. It is all about love,
and communion ensures a constant flow of God's covenant
love to us as we remember what He has done.

Communion is a celebration of God's love for us. It is much
more powerful than many believers realize. An example is
the area of physical healing. In receiving communion, we are
"proclaiming the Lord's death" until He comes. What does that
mean? It means we are declaring that by the death of Jesus
we are healed and the curse has been removed from us. We
aren't just consuming a piece of bread or cup of juice. We are
receiving spiritual life and every benefit that has been assigned
to us by the death of Jesus. What a powerful blessing!

Communion is also a time of recommitting ourselves to the
covenant relationship with Jesus. Remember, covenant means
"to cut." It is a sacrificial, permanent relationship. Communion

is a time for each of us to consider if something else has taken God's place in our lives and if we have compromised our relationship with Him in any way. If yes, we must be willing to either do away with it or put it in its right place. This is a constant process in our relationship with the Lord that keeps our relationship dynamic and intimate.

When I take communion, I begin by reminding myself of God's grace and love for me. In the natural, I never feel worthy to receive communion—because I'm not. Every blessing of God is because of His grace and mercy. That is what communion is all about. The devil knows how to ruin every good moment with God by simply making it about us and our sins and mistakes. I will not let him do this because it isn't about me—it is about Jesus. His death removed my sins forever and paved the way for me to enter into the presence of God without shame or fear.

After focusing on God's love and grace, I celebrate the benefits of Jesus' body and blood. I remember that He has removed the curses of sickness, poverty, death, and bondage from my life as He has restored His blessings to me. As I receive the bread of communion, I receive the full blessings of God as my inheritance in Him. If I have a sickness or any other problem, I believe God for healing and restoration. I have had many powerful encounters with God's healing grace during communion.

As I receive the communion cup, I remember that Jesus died for my sins. I celebrate as I remember that I am forgiven and have unhindered access to the Lord in an intimate, personal relationship. I remind myself that because of Jesus' blood, God is now my best Friend and loving Father. I am forever forgiven and justified before God because of the finished work of Jesus on the cross.

Communion is one of the most sacred traditions of the Christian faith. Along with water baptism, communion is an act of covenant keeping with God that is very significant and releases His special blessings as often as we do it.

I believe communion should be observed regularly. Churches differ in how often they serve communion, and some churches use wine while others use grape juice. Both are symbolic of Christ's blood, and both are fine.

You don't have to be served communion at church or by a pastor or spiritual leader. You can take communion on your own. I think it is very special to do this as a married couple, as a family, or in times of special need—especially in times of sickness. Communion is powerful to invoke healing and to declare the benefits of the Lord's death as an outward sign of faith and obedience.

Along those lines, I recommend a powerful book for you. It is called *Health and Wholeness Through the Holy Communion* by Joseph Prince. In this book, he spells out how God ministers healing to us as we receive communion. The book is easy to read and understand, and it really brings to light how powerful communion is meant to be.

As a believer in Christ, you have entered into the most sacred and special covenant relationship on earth. God is totally committed to you and will never leave you or forsake you (Hebrews 13:5). His covenant love is the basis of your hope and peace, and you can count on it forever.

Water baptism is the covenant seal of our relationship with Christ. It is the public acknowledgement of the private act of making Jesus the Lord of our lives. It is a onetime act and does not need to be repeated.

Communion is the ongoing covenant sign of our relationship with the Lord. It should occur regularly—we need to remind ourselves often of what Jesus has done for us as we frequently examine our lives and recommit ourselves to Him.

Keeping the covenants of baptism and communion is a big step toward Christ. Now you're ready for the next one!

3

Baptism in the Holy Spirit

Being assembled together with *them,* He commanded them not to depart from Jerusalem, but to wait for the Promise of the Father, "which," *He said,* "you have heard from Me; for John truly baptized with water, but you shall be baptized with the Holy Spirit not many days from now." Therefore, when they had come together, they asked Him, saying, "Lord, will You at this time restore the kingdom to Israel?" And He said to them, "It is not for you to know times or seasons which the Father has put in His own authority. But you shall receive power when the Holy Spirit has come upon you; and you shall be witnesses to Me in Jerusalem, and in all Judea and Samaria, and to the end of the earth."

—Acts 1:4–8

I can honestly say that when I received Christ, I had never heard of the Holy Spirit. I never heard about Him in a church service or Sunday school class or any other environment, except that I vaguely recall the "Holy Ghost" being sung about in the doxology at the end of the church service. But as I read the Bible on my own, I came across Scriptures like those in Acts 1.

I was always fascinated when I read Scriptures about the Holy Spirit that promised power and other super-natural blessings that I really wanted to experience. The following are some examples of the Scriptures about the Holy Spirit that I read as a young believer and that piqued my interest:

"I will pray the Father, and He will give you another Helper, that He may abide with you forever—the Spirit of truth, whom the world cannot receive, because it neither sees Him nor knows Him; but you know Him, for He dwells with you and will be in you" (John 14:16–17).

"The Helper, the Holy Spirit, whom the Father will send in My name, He will teach you all things, and bring to your remembrance all things that I said to you" (John 14:26).

"When the Helper comes, whom I shall send to you from the Father, the Spirit of truth who proceeds from the Father, He will testify of Me" (John 15:26).

"When He, the Spirit of truth, has come, He will guide you into all truth; for He will not speak on His own *authority*, but whatever He hears He will speak; and He will tell you things to come. He will glorify Me, for He will take of what is Mine and declare *it* to you" (John 16:13–14).

The manifestation of the Spirit is given to each one for the profit *of all:* for to one is given the word of wisdom through the Spirit, to another the word of knowledge through the same Spirit, to another faith by the same Spirit, to another gifts of healings by the same Spirit, to another the working of miracles, to another prophecy, to another discerning of spirits, to another *different* kinds of tongues, to another the interpretation of tongues. But one and the same Spirit works all these things, distributing to each one individually as He wills.

For as the body is one and has many members, but all the members of that one body, being many, are one body, so also *is* Christ. For by one Spirit we were all baptized into one body—whether Jews or Greeks, whether slaves or free—and have all been made to drink into one Spirit (1 Corinthians 12:7–13).

These are just a few examples of Scriptures where the Bible refers to the coming of the Holy Spirit and what He would accomplish in believers' lives. Notice that Jesus often referred to the Holy Spirit as "the Helper," which is also translated as "Comforter." It is the Greek word *parakletos*. It means someone who walks alongside us to help us.

For me, one of the most intriguing things the Bible referred to about the Holy Spirit was something called the baptism of the Holy Spirit.

Immersed in the Spirit

Remember the Scripture at the beginning of this chapter from Acts 1? In that passage Jesus promised the disciples that the Holy Spirit would give them power when they were baptized into Him. He spoke this to them 40 days after His resurrection and just before He ascended into heaven. Ten days later, at the Feast of Pentecost, the Holy Spirit fell, transforming the disciples' lives. Here is the account:

When the Day of Pentecost had fully come, they were all with one accord in one place. And suddenly there came a sound from heaven, as of a rushing mighty wind, and it filled the whole house where they were sitting. Then there appeared to them divided tongues, as of fire, and *one* sat upon each of them. And they were all filled with the Holy Spirit and began to speak with other tongues, as the Spirit gave them utterance.

And there were dwelling in Jerusalem Jews, devout men, from every nation under heaven. And when this sound occurred, the multitude came together, and were confused, because everyone heard them speak in his own language. Then they were all amazed and marveled, saying to one another, "Look, are not all these who speak Galileans? And how *is it that* we hear, each in our own language in which we were born? Parthians and Medes and Elamites, those dwelling in Mesopotamia, Judea and Cappadocia, Pontus and Asia, Phrygia and Pamphylia, Egypt and the parts of Libya adjoining Cyrene, visitors from Rome, both Jews and proselytes, Cretans and Arabs—we hear them speaking in our own tongues the wonderful works of God." So they were all amazed and perplexed, saying to one another, "Whatever could this mean?"

Others mocking said, "They are full of new wine."

But Peter, standing up with the eleven, raised his voice and said to them, "Men of Judea and all who dwell in Jerusalem, let this be known to you, and heed my words. For these are not drunk, as you suppose, since it is *only* the third hour of the day. But this is what was spoken by the prophet Joel:

'*And it shall come to pass in the last days, says God,*
That I will pour out of My Spirit on all flesh;
Your sons and your daughters shall prophesy,
Your young men shall see visions,

Your old men shall dream dreams.
And on My menservants and on My maidservants
I will pour out My Spirit in those days;
And they shall prophesy'" (Acts 2:1–18).

Jesus commanded His disciples (who were already saved) to wait in Jerusalem until they were filled with power. He told them that once they received the Holy Spirit, they would be empowered to be His witnesses to the uttermost parts of the earth.

The baptism of the Holy Spirit is about immersing us into an empowering relationship with the Holy Spirit so we can fully know and serve God. The Holy Spirit is God and is equal with God the Son and God the Father. He always speaks and acts in accordance with the nature and Word of God.

Thus, once we are saved and baptized in water, there is still another essential step we must take to live a successful Christian life—we must be baptized in the Holy Spirit. It is an experience subsequent to (after) salvation. It may happen 10 minutes, 10 days, 10 months, or 10 years after we get saved, but it doesn't happen just because we are saved.

Being saved is about accepting Jesus' Lordship. It is about the forgiveness of sins and eternal life. Baptism in the Holy Spirit is about living for God in this life and having the assistance of God every day to know Him, overcome sin, and accomplish His will. We cannot do it on our own. We must have the continual partnership of the Holy Spirit. That is why Jesus spoke of Him so often and commanded the disciples to wait for Him.

How I Received the Baptism of the Holy Spirit

As I stated earlier, when I got saved and water-baptized, I was never told about the Holy Spirit. For the first several years of my Christian walk, I was a devoted follower of Christ, trying to do my best to please God. However, I felt I just couldn't do it. I was constantly disappointed in my inability to "do the do's and not do the don'ts." I also struggled to understand the Bible and to pray. I disciplined myself to pray and read my Bible every day, but I felt like I could never break through and really connect with God at the level I desired.

As I read about the Holy Spirit in the Bible, I was interested in experiencing what Jesus spoke about. I knew I needed power. I also wanted to be guided into truth and receive revelation about the Scriptures. When Jesus referred to the Holy Spirit as the "Spirit of Truth" and promised that He would lead us into all truth, I thought, *Yes, that is what I need*!

I also read in different parts of the Bible about people speaking in tongues when they received the Holy Spirit. I didn't know what that meant, but I was interested to know more. In our Sunday school class at church one weekend, I asked my teacher about the baptism of the Holy Spirit and speaking in tongues. He became embarrassed and couldn't answer my question.

I didn't know that my church didn't believe in the baptism of the Holy Spirit, speaking in tongues, or the contemporary operation of the gifts of the Holy Spirit, such as healing and prophecy. (1 Corinthians 12 and 14 explain the gifts of the Holy Spirit and their operation in believers' lives and in the church.) I was troubled that my teacher was embarrassed by something that was clearly in the Bible.

After the class, a woman approached my wife, Karen, and told her that she was baptized in the Holy Spirit and spoke in tongues. We became close friends with her and her husband as they took us under their wings and even invited us to some Christian meetings where the Holy Spirit was talked about and manifestations of the gifts of the Holy Spirit were in operation.

All of this led to Karen and me receiving the baptism of the Holy Spirit not long after that. I can tell you that it transformed my life, and more than 40 years later, it is still as real and powerful as on the first day. Before receiving the baptism of the Holy Spirit, I felt inadequate and as though I couldn't understand the Bible or connect with God in prayer. However, all that changed!

I now felt that I knew God intimately. The Holy Spirit was revealing Jesus to me, just as Jesus said He would in John 15:26.

With the Spirit of Truth leading me, I could now understand the Bible. After all, He did inspire all of the Bible writers and knows better than anyone else what the Bible means.

I now had the power to do the do's and not do the don'ts. I wasn't perfect, but I was changed. Just as Pentecost transformed Peter from the coward who denied Christ just weeks earlier into a bold proclaimer of the gospel, so I was changed and could do things that were previously not possible for me.

My personality also began to change into that of a more peaceful and loving person. The fruit of the Holy Spirit's personality, as described in Galatians 5:22–23, began to manifest in me. I became a better husband, father, and representative of Christ as the rough edges of my temperament wore away.

I began speaking in tongues, the first of many other gifts I have operated in over the years. The speaking in tongues I am referring to is a private prayer language, born of the Spirit to help us (see Romans 8:26 and 1 Corinthians 14:2–5, 14–15). There are other expressions of speaking in tongues that are public in nature and for other purposes. These are found in Acts 2:4–8 (the miracle of foreign languages spoken by those who don't know them) and 1 Corinthians 14:5–13 (tongues with an interpretation in a church setting that is a prophetic utterance). I have never seen the miracle of languages in operation but have heard reports about it from people on the mission field. I have seen tongues with interpretation occur many times in a manner that was edifying in a group setting. I have prayed privately in tongues virtually every day for the past 40 years. Early in my experience, I was warned by some who didn't believe in tongues that it was of the devil. I can assure you that it isn't. I feel closer to God when I pray in tongues (1 Corinthians 14:2–5). It has been an incredible blessing in my life.

My testimony is matched by millions of others over the centuries who have received the baptism of the Holy Spirit.

Questions About Receiving the Baptism of the Holy Spirit

Here are some answers to important questions that people frequently ask about the baptism of the Holy Spirit.

How do I receive the baptism of the Holy Spirit?

You receive the baptism of the Holy Spirit simply by asking and receiving through faith—just as you received Jesus when you were saved. The Holy Spirit is a free gift of God; you don't have to deserve Him. When we need Him the most, we deserve Him the least. That is why it is so wonderful to know that He is the Spirit of grace.

It might help to read these Scriptures: Luke 11:13; Galatians 3:1–14; and Zechariah 12:10.

Can anything keep a person from receiving the baptism of the Holy Spirit?

Yes, there are three main reasons why people are unsuccessful in experiencing the baptism of the Holy Spirit: unbelief, unforgiveness toward others, and unconfessed sin. We must receive the Holy Spirit by faith as we deal with sin in our lives. The Holy Spirit is extremely gracious but remember—His first name is Holy. I encourage you to read about the importance of faith in Galatians 3:1–14 (if you haven't already), as well as Acts 8:9–2. This second passage deals with a man who couldn't receive the Holy Spirit because of bitterness and unrepentant sin.

Didn't I receive the Holy Spirit when I was saved?
Why do I have to receive Him again?

At salvation, we are born again by the Holy Spirit, just as I explained in Chapter 1. Every believer has been born again of the Holy Spirit. However, even though the disciples in Acts 1, including Peter, were saved, they were also commanded to wait in Jerusalem to receive the baptism of the Holy Spirit. Here are some other Scriptures telling about saved people who later received the baptism of the Holy Spirit: Acts 8:12–17 and 19:1–6.

The issue at salvation is Jesus. Baptism in the Holy Spirit, however, is about the Holy Spirit and allowing Him to immerse us into His fullness and empower us to know and serve God. It is a separate experience because it is a separate decision. It doesn't have to be a long time after we are saved. In fact, it shouldn't be. But like me, many people who are genuinely saved are never told about the importance of the baptism of the Holy Spirit. Others are told they don't need the baptism of the Holy Spirit because they already have Him if they are saved.

Yes, every saved person has the Holy Spirit, but let me use this analogy to distinguish between salvation and baptism in the Holy Spirit: Salvation is taking a drink of living water that resurrects the spirit inside you. Baptism in the Holy Spirit is jumping into the lake where that water came from to fully empower your total being. Since I have experienced both, I can tell you about it better than a person who hasn't experienced baptism in the Holy Spirit.

Do I have to speak in tongues to be saved or
to be baptized in the Holy Spirit?

No. I know of many godly, Spirit-filled people who don't speak in tongues. I have also known people through the years who speak in tongues but are weird and don't live as they should. Just because someone does or doesn't speak in tongues doesn't alone declare his spiritual status.

Having said that, I want to state that I believe speaking in tongues is an incredible blessing as a private prayer language. As the apostle Paul says in 1 Corinthians 14:18, "I thank my God I speak with tongues more than you all." Try it when you are alone and are asking the Holy Spirit to baptize you. He won't force you to do anything, including speaking in tongues. You will have to do it by faith as He prompts you.

Some people fear speaking in tongues or yielding completely to the Holy Spirit out of concern they might lose control and become fanatics. It is just the opposite. *Self-control* is listed in Galatians 5:22–23 as one of the fruits (characteristics or personality traits) of the Holy Spirit. The more Spirit-filled you are, the more you are in control of your behavior.

Paul also emphasizes this point in 1 Corinthians 14:32–33 in reference to those who minister the gifts of the Holy Spirit in church: "The spirits of the prophets are subject to the prophets. For God is not *the author* of confusion but of peace, as in all the churches of the saints." The phrase "the spirits of the prophets are subject to the prophets" could also be put like this: "You are in control of your own behavior when you are ministering in the spiritual gifts."

You can't do weird things and blame them on the Holy Spirit. He never causes disorderly or unbecoming conduct. Even though there are always fanatics and weirdos doing flaky things and attributing them to the Holy Spirit, it isn't truly of the Spirit of God. The Holy Spirit is gentle, gracious, and orderly in how He operates. Everything about Him is a blessing, and you never need fear Him.

When you yield your tongue to God, He can use you in a more powerful manner. Our tongues have the power of life and death in them (Proverbs 18:21), and if our tongues are not surrendered to the Lord, He simply can't use us as He desires. Conversely, when our tongues are surrendered to God and yielded to the Holy Spirit, it leads to a dimension of spiritual experience and ministry that was previously unknown. This is my testimony and that of many others I know who speak in tongues.

I would strongly encourage you to yield your tongue to the Holy Spirit and give Him the opportunity to impart this special gift to you.

Why do I need to pray in tongues?

Speaking in tongues is primarily expressed as a private prayer language. So why do we need it?

First of all, praying in tongues vastly expands our ability to pray as we should. Romans 8:26 says this about the Holy Spirit:

> The Spirit also helps in our weaknesses. For we do not know what we should pray for as we ought, but the Spirit Himself makes intercession for us with groanings which cannot be uttered.

The "groanings" Paul speaks of are simply words that originate in our spirits and that our natural minds cannot understand.

Here is the simplest way to understand praying in tongues: it is recognizing our mental and spiritual inabilities to pray as we should and allowing the Holy Spirit to help us. When you do not pray in tongues, you are limited in how you can pray. For example, let's say you are praying, and you are unaware that one of your close relatives is about to have a life-threatening heart attack. Even though you don't know about it, the Holy Spirit does. He knows everything. As you are praying only for those things you understand, you are very limited. However, when you recognize your weakness and allow the Holy Spirit to help you, He will pray with you and through you through tongues. In other words, as you are praying in tongues, you could actually be praying for your relative's heart and not even know it. How wonderful that the Holy Spirit would help us in this manner!

Here is how the apostle Paul describes this in 1 Corinthians 14:

> He who speaks in a tongue does not speak to men but to God, for no one understands *him*; however, in the spirit he speaks mysteries (v.2).
>
> If I pray in a tongue, my spirit prays, but my understanding is unfruitful. What is *the conclusion* then? I will pray with the spirit, and I will also pray with the under-

standing. I will sing with the spirit, and I will also sing
with the understanding (vv. 14–15).

I thank my God I speak with tongues more than you all
(v. 18).

Paul clearly says that we should pray in tongues ("with the
spirit") as well as with our understanding. He also tells us
that he sang in the spirit and with his understanding.

Beyond giving us divine empowerment to pray beyond
our human understanding, the Holy Spirit also leads us into
a greater intimacy with God. This is the second important
reason for praying in tongues. Even though our minds may
be "unfruitful" as we pray or praise in tongues, our spirits are
edified and blessed.

I have prayed and praised in tongues thousands of times.
Every time, I feel closer to God and spiritually blessed.

The Holy Spirit will always lead us closer to God. Speaking
in tongues allows Him to guide us on a higher spiritual level
than we could ever achieve on our own. The benefit is greater
effectiveness in prayer and a closer, more intimate relationship with God.

Is baptism in the Holy Spirit a onetime experience or something I must do often?

There is an initial experience of being baptized in the Holy
Spirit that occurs when we ask for and receive Him by faith.
However, once we are baptized in the Spirit, we must yield to
Him daily, even moment by moment, for His power and grace
to flow through us (Ephesians 5:18–19).

Someone once asked me, "Why do we have to keep getting
filled with the Spirit?"

My answer was this: "We leak!"

We live in a sinful world, and life is demanding. Just as we must drink water constantly to stay physically hydrated, especially when it is hot, we must also keep asking the Holy Spirit to fill us to stay spiritually hydrated, especially in demanding times. Just like it doesn't matter today how good the water was that I drank last week, so it also doesn't matter how good my experience was in the Holy Spirit last week if I'm not experiencing Him currently. If we don't drink regularly of water and of the Holy Spirit, we will dry up and begin to perish.

The main thing to remember is this: the Holy Spirit doesn't want to be an impersonal power source in our battery of life. He wants to be a supernatural Friend, walking beside us in a real, dynamic relationship. Love is the reason He is in our lives. If we don't realize that, we will never truly understand Him or relate to Him properly.

Do I have to feel something in order to be baptized in the Holy Spirit?

Not necessarily. Our emotions are fickle and can't be trusted as a barometer of spiritual experience or truth. We must receive the Holy Spirit by faith. Having said that, however, I would also say that the baptism of the Holy Spirit should make a real difference in a person's life.

On the night I received the baptism of the Holy Spirit, I felt heat from my head downward through my body. In my heart I saw Jesus hanging on the cross, and I knew He had died for me and loved me with a love I had never known before. My experience was emotional, spiritual, mental, and physical.

God knows you intimately and knows how to speak your language. Everyone experiences the baptism of the Holy Spirit in some unique manner but with common manifestations (love, power, peace, revelation, tongues, and so on). Ask the Holy Spirit into your life and receive Him by faith. Don't gauge the reality of the experience by your emotions alone. Gauge it mainly by how it affects your relationship with Christ and your ability to live for Him. Baptism in the Holy Spirit doesn't make us perfect, and it doesn't make life easy at all times. However, it does make us more like Jesus, and it makes living for Him possible and exciting. Here is a prayer for you to pray if you want to receive the baptism of the Holy Spirit and take this important spiritual step:

> Father, thank You for the promise of the Holy Spirit and for sending Him into my life. I repent of my sins and forgive everyone who has hurt me, has sinned against me, or has hurt my loved ones. By faith, I now ask You to baptize me in Your Holy Spirit. I surrender my life to live for You. Holy Spirit, come into my life and fill me. Baptize me in Your presence and power and lead me daily. I surrender completely to You and ask You to lead me closer to Jesus and empower me to live victoriously for Him. I pray that You will impart spiritual gifts into my life and use me to glorify God and help others. I also surrender my tongue to You and pray that You will give me a personal prayer language to enable me to pray more effectively. In Jesus' name, Amen.

You might also want a pastor or church leader to pray for you. There is a biblical principle of the importance of the laying on of hands, especially as it relates to the impartation of the Holy Spirit (Acts 8:17; 19:6; Hebrews 6:1–2). It isn't always necessary, but on the night I received the baptism of the Holy Spirit, I had earlier been prayed for by a leader who was Spirit-baptized and who had laid his hands on me in faith.

You've now finished taking three huge steps toward Christ. Our journey continues as we take step four in the next chapter.

4

Christian Fellowship

As iron sharpens iron,
So a man sharpens the countenance of his friend.

—Proverbs 27:17

When I was growing up, my experience in church wasn't good. In fact, I developed an attitude toward Christians—I thought they were nerds. There were some Christians I liked, but as a group, I thought they were boring, and I didn't want to be around them.

On the other hand, I grew up with a large group of friends I really liked.

Most of us considered ourselves "Christians" and went to church on some regular basis. But church never changed how we lived. We were rebellious and ungodly in our behavior. We smoked, drank, cursed, and were immoral.

Karen had a much better group of friends than I did.

While I was living in rebellion and immorality, Karen was going to Bible studies and growing in the Lord. Even though we loved each other and planned on getting married, we were growing apart spiritually. As I stated earlier, everything came to a head when I had sex with a girl at my bachelor party one week before Karen and I were supposed to get married. It was the breaking point in our relationship and the turning point in my life.

The morning after my bachelor party was when I received Christ into my heart and made Him Lord of my life. Even though I was just saved, I heard the Lord speak to me that morning. A few minutes after praying the prayer to receive Christ, I heard a voice in my heart say, "Never see your friends again." It was clear to me that God was giving me a directive to break relations with my friends.

I want to use my experience as an introduction to the importance of having the right kinds of friends—and not having the wrong kinds.

Breaking Off the Wrong Friendships

The day I was saved, I was supposed to have baseball practice with all of my friends. I was the captain of our baseball team and had all of our equipment in the trunk of my car. I felt great about my commitment to the Lord, and I knew that what I had heard the Lord speak to me was right.

That afternoon, I pulled up to the baseball field where our team met for practice. As soon as I pulled up, my friends gathered around my car. I opened my trunk and started putting the equipment on the sidewalk. As I was doing that, my friends began laughing and making comments about my bachelor party the night before.

All of them were celebratory about the fact that girls were there and most of us had sex with them. As they congratulated me on my conquest, I'm sure they could tell I was less than excited. With them surrounding the trunk of my car, I turned to them and said, "I didn't like what happened last night, and I'm not going to do that type of thing again."

When I said those words, their celebration stopped.

One of my friends asked, "Evans, what do you mean? Last night was great!"

I replied, "No, it wasn't great. I cheated on Karen, and I didn't want to do that. I'm going to live my life for the Lord from now on. I'm also not going to be on the baseball team any longer, so one of you will need to be the captain."

When I said that, the tone of the conversation changed immediately. Someone asked if I was going to tell Karen what had happened. (They knew that if Karen found out, all of their girlfriends would also know.) I told them I was going to tell Karen as soon as I left them.

As one of my friends tried to talk me out of it, the others started grabbing the baseball equipment off the sidewalk and walking away. I looked at the one trying to talk me out of it and told him I was going to tell Karen and there was nothing he could do to change it. Having heard that, he walked away to join the others.

Except for running into them in restaurants or other public places, I never saw those friends again.

Karen and I ended up marrying a week later, and except for Karen and Jesus, I was friendless. I really wanted friends, but I knew Karen and the Lord didn't want me to have close friends who weren't Christians—true Christians. So I just didn't have any male friends for quite a while.

Establishing the Right Friendships

During the first year of our marriage, Karen and I went to church on a pretty regular basis. It was a good influence on us. I tried to stay to myself as much as possible, but Karen wanted us to get more involved and build relationships with other couples in our church. So, I reluctantly went with her to a Sunday school class for young couples. I was really uncomfortable in that group.

I thought the guys were nerdy and fake. This was my worst nightmare. I thought to myself, *Well, I gave my life to Jesus, and I'm not turning back. But these Christians are a test!* Even though we started attending that Sunday school class regularly, I kept things cordial and didn't pursue close relationships.

That all changed the day I asked the question about the baptism of the Holy Spirit and speaking in tongues. One of the young ladies told Karen after class that she and her husband had experienced the baptism of the Holy Spirit. Shortly thereafter, we went to dinner with them, and we found our first close Christian relationships.

As soon as I got to know them, I felt bad that I had judged them as I had. They were great. He was really fun and also loved the Lord. He was the first true Christian male friend I could be around and really enjoy myself. Karen and I loved being around them, and they became close friends of ours.

Today we have many wonderful Christian friends. I have totally changed my mind about Christians and church. I truly believe Christians are the best friends on earth. They are fun, they encourage you and help you do the right thing, and they are faithful in bad times.

Not every Christian is this way, and not every church is a good church. But I can tell you that for you to grow in Christ and be successful in your desire to live for Him, fellowship with other believers is essential. Without a committed relationship to a local church and fellow believers, you will not be able to succeed in your personal walk with Christ or in your call to serve the Lord.

Why Choosing Your Friends Carefully Matters

Having been a Christian now for more than 40 years, I have seen the life cycle of thousands of believers I have known personally. In every single case in which a believer lives a dynamic and successful life over a long period of time, he or she has close, accountable relationships with a local church and other believers. I have never seen an exception. It is essential, especially in the evil world in which we live.

My heart has been broken many times over the years as I have witnessed the fall of intelligent, gifted, and wonderful Christian people who either wouldn't break off unhealthy relationships or wouldn't commit to church and developing healthy relationships with other believers. I have also realized that it doesn't matter how talented, mature, or dedicated people are; once they are isolated or in the wrong crowd, they are in danger and will inevitably fail spiritually if they don't change.

My first major heartbreak concerning this issue was with the friend I mentioned earlier—the first Christian friend I had whom I really liked. He was a strong believer and had a positive influence on me for years until he moved away to another city. As soon as he moved, I noticed a change in him for the worse.

During a phone conversation one day, my friend began telling me about his new boss. He was a wealthy man and was very ungodly. My friend had to travel with him a lot for business. On these business trips he was influenced by his boss to do things he would have never done before. Also, he stopped going to church.

When I saw the changes happening in my friend, I questioned him about it on more than one occasion. When I did, he told me that he was in a different season in his Christian life and God was using him to evangelize his boss. Baloney! After a few more months, he left his wife and children to live a life of full-blown immorality.

You must understand that you will always become like the people closest to you. Here is how the apostle Paul puts it in 1 Corinthians 15:33: "Do not be deceived: Evil company corrupts good habits." Notice that he says it is the negative that has greater power than the positive when you are in close relationship ("company") with them. If you have good habits, bad company will corrupt them. If you don't believe this, you are deceived.

Concerning close relationships with people who are not actively practicing the Christian faith, Paul gives this command:

Do not be unequally yoked together with unbelievers.
For what fellowship has righteousness with lawlessness?
And what communion has light with darkness? And what
accord has Christ with Belial? Or what part has a believer
with an unbeliever? And what agreement has the temple
of God with idols? For you are the temple of the living
God. As God has said:

"I will dwell in them
And walk among them.
I will be their God,
And they shall be My people."

Therefore

"'Come out from among them
And be separate,' says the Lord.
'Do not touch what is unclean,
And I will receive you.
I will be a Father to you,
And you shall be My sons and daughters,'
Says the Lord Almighty" (2 Corinthians 6:14–18).

When Paul speaks of being unequally *yoked*, he is speaking
of the farming implement that binds two animals, such as
oxen, together to unite them for a task such as plowing. He
uses this metaphor to warn us that we are not to be engaged
in entangling, binding relationships with those who are not
believers in Christ. This includes all close relationships and
especially the marriage relationship. This does not mean that
you should divorce your spouse if you receive Christ and your
spouse does not. You should remain married to him or her.
It does mean, though, that as a single person you should not
date or marry an unbeliever.

All of us know people in our families or neighborhoods and at school or work who aren't believers and who have unrighteous behavior. We can love and befriend these people—and we should. However, they cannot be the source of our closest fellowship and friendships. Our closest relationships need to be with believers who share our values and our commitment to Christ. From that foundation we can then reach out to others and befriend them without the fear of them influencing us negatively.

The author of Hebrews writes a word of caution:

> Let us consider one another in order to stir up love and good works, not forsaking the assembling of ourselves together, as *is* the manner of some, but exhorting one another, and so much the more as you see the Day approaching (Hebrews 10:24–25).

This is a very important text of Scripture because it not only exhorts us to assemble together regularly with other believers but also tells us why: we need to encourage one another and stir each other up to love God and others and serve the Lord faithfully.

We live in an evil world. We need the constant love and encouragement of church and friendships with practicing Christians. Without it, we simply cannot withstand the forces of temptation, deception, and persecution that are in the world today. With a strong foundation of fellowship, not only can we make it, but we can also make a difference in the lives of others and lead them to Christ. This is the highest purpose of our call as believers.

How to Make and Maintain Christian Friendships

As you take the step to break off unhealthy relationships and get involved in church and Christian relationships, here are some important keys:

Look for sincerity and adherence to Scripture, not perfection.

If you are too idealistic in looking for the perfect church or Christian friends, you will be constantly disappointed. The best church in the world is full of imperfect people and will experience ups and downs. The same is true of all Christians. You need to pray for God to guide you as you seek out the right church and Christian friends. Begin visiting churches and see what happens in your heart as you attend them.

Don't ever choose a church that is legalistic and condemning—one where people feel they are better than others and treat sinful people like the enemy. Also, don't choose a church that waters down the Bible or refuses to take a stand for truth. A good church is always a balance of truth and grace. Extremes are dangerous.

You might have to look around for a while before you find the church you feel that God is leading you to. You will almost always see things in the church you choose that you wish were different. That is normal. But you must have faith and confidence in your heart that God has led you there. Once you have that faith, then commit. Be a faithful member of that church.

The same is true with Christian friends. None of them are perfect, but you can know the difference between those who are sincere and those who are not. For example, in my early Christian walk, I knew a man who came to church and acted as though he was a man of extraordinary faith. However, he wouldn't work and instead relied on donations from people in the church to provide for his wife and children. He was in sin and insincere (2 Thessalonians 3:10). I was kind to him but avoided having a close relationship with him.

I have also known people in church who were immoral, rebellious, gossipy, and crooked in business dealings. I try to be kind to people and not judge them. However, I avoid relationships with people who I believe will be a negative influence on me. By the way, I'm not judging them based on hearsay. I'm careful not to believe rumors or act on what others might say. I'm talking about things I know to be true.

Again, regardless of whether people identify themselves as believers or nonbelievers, you will become like the people you are close to. All of my close friends are imperfect but sincere. I am also imperfect but sincere. I need grace from my friends just as much as they need grace from me. However, none of us excuse behavior in our lives that is sinful or corrupt. We are committed to growing in our faith and being accountable to one another.

Be a part of "big church" and "little church."

Here is what the book of Acts says about the early church: "Continuing daily with one accord in the temple, and breaking bread from house to house, they ate their food with gladness and simplicity of heart" (Acts 2:46).

Notice that the early Christians went from the temple (the church assembly where everyone was together—"big church") to individual houses where they experienced more intimate fellowship ("little church"). They had large, corporate meetings and small-group gatherings on a regular basis. I believe this should be the pattern for every church and believer. We experience God in a powerful way as we meet corporately, and we experience rich Christian fellowship when we meet in small groups. Both are essential.

You will also find that some of your best Christian friendships develop out of small-group fellowship. These are groups like Sunday school classes, Bible studies, small-group gatherings in homes, and so on.

Don't let fear or self-consciousness keep you from church or close Christian fellowship.

Before joining the staff of the church where I pastored for many years, I was a member. Karen and I started attending Trinity Fellowship in Amarillo, Texas, in 1979 when I was a businessman. I loved the church but felt I was the most unspiritual person in it.

When we first started attending, we sat in the back row. I was very self-conscious. I saw how others worshipped the Lord and interacted with one another, and even though I really enjoyed the atmosphere of the church and the people, I was afraid someone was going to find out how spiritually immature and messed up I was. In spite of my fears, though, people were nothing but gracious and kind to me.

After we had been attending the church for a few months, Karen signed us up for a discipleship class that met in a home.

I didn't want to go. I had just gotten used to coming to church and felt safe in the larger group. I feared that in the smaller group they would discover who I really was and that it would be embarrassing.

With a lot of prayer and coaxing from Karen, we ended up going to the group. There were thirteen people, including us. On the first night, the leader, Bob Key, asked if anyone played the guitar and could be the worship leader for the group. Karen immediately told Bob that I played the guitar and could do it. I thought I was going to die (or kill her)!

To make a long story short, we fell in love with that group, and it created a huge breakthrough in our spiritual lives. The leaders of the group, Bob and Sarah, became dear friends of ours for many years. They have now both gone to be with the Lord, but they made an eternal investment in our lives.

I remember so well the fears I had of getting involved and being exposed with all of my hang-ups and problems. I now realize everyone has problems, and we all start at the same place. The devil loves to use fear and comparison to keep us from getting involved in church and committed Christian relationships.

I am so thankful that Karen encouraged me to get involved and press past my fears. It was the key to me taking the crucial step that resulted in finding our wonderful church home and true Christian friendships. It was also the key that caused me to grow in my faith and become who I am today.

I encourage you to be open with a leader or mature Christian friend if you are struggling with an addiction, besetting sin, or particular problem that you cannot get freedom from on your own. We all need support and accountability in these times. Don't be ashamed. Everyone deals with these types of issues at some point, especially when we are beginning our walk with Christ as new believers. Don't tell everyone your problems, though. Find a pastor, leader, mature friend, or small group that offers a confidential and supportive atmosphere to help you in the area you are struggling with. This would include marriage and family issues.

Don't let offenses or disappointments cause you to separate from church or your Christian friends.

It is inevitable that in the course of being involved in a church or with Christian friends, you are going to be disappointed and hurt. There is no such thing as a close relationship in which it doesn't happen. You have to have realistic expectations and be willing to work at the relationship and persevere through challenging times.

You must also understand that the devil is an accuser (Revelation 12:10) and a slanderer (Ephesians 4:27—"devil" is interpreted as "slanderer"). His full-time job is to make us offended at God, our family members, our church, and our Christian friends. He hates godly, wholesome, healthy relationships, so he is always trying to produce intrigue and division.

For us to be a part of committed, long-term relationships, we must expect problems and deal with them in a biblical and mature manner. On many occasions when we are hurt and disappointed, we can just pray through it. The problem involved isn't that big of a deal, and we can endure it with God's grace. We must learn to pray for our pastor, church leaders, fellow members, and Christian friends. It is the answer to most issues (1 John 5:16–17).

On other occasions, though, prayer isn't enough. We must speak the truth in love to those involved and talk things out (Ephesians 4:15). I have done this hundreds of times over the years and have found it to be crucial in developing and maintaining healthy relationships. When I first did this, I feared confrontation and actually dreaded it. Now I don't fear it at all. I have found it to be liberating and a key to great relationships.

So often when I have been hurt or disappointed, I think I know what is going on, but talking things out has proved to me that I really don't know until I speak to the others involved. In 90 percent of the cases where I speak the truth in love to others, the situation resolves itself, and things are better than before. In the other 10 percent, it is still better to have talked about it, though things may not have worked out as I wished. (By the way, any time you go to confront someone, you must be gracious and humble and be willing to take responsibility for your own problems and mistakes.)

The worst situations are those in which serious sin is involved and the leader or friend will not repent or acknowledge his wrongdoing. Again, we need to deal with what we know to be true and not hearsay. But there are times when a church leader or friend commits a serious moral, legal, or spiritual sin and must be confronted.

It is always best if church leaders address these kinds of issues in accordance with Matthew 18:15–17. Sometimes, however, they won't. That doesn't keep us from doing the right thing as we speak the truth in love and seek information and reconciliation. If there truly is serious sin involved and if the guilty parties confess and repent, we should forgive them and celebrate. If they don't, we should break off close relations with them until they repent, even though we still love and pray for them.

If the sin is with the pastor or key leadership of the church and if the leadership of the church won't address it, we might have to consider leaving the church. We should be careful before taking this step. We should be committed to church and friends and not take steps of separation hastily. We should separate only after much prayer and true attempts to reconcile.

Don't let busyness or distraction keep you from church or Christian fellowship.

There is a saying that I like: "If the devil can't get in front of you and stop you, he will get behind you and push you too fast."

We live in a fast-paced world that is getting faster every day. Research has shown that families today are spending less time together than ever before because of the individual stresses and outside opportunities they experience. Even children today are more stressed than ever.

Karen and I made the decision many years ago that church and Christian friends were an inviolable priority in our lives. Other things may have to go, but under no circumstances will we compromise our relationship with our church or Christian friends. We are so thankful that we have taken this stance.

Christian fellowship has been an anchor in the midst of the stresses and difficulties in our lives. It has been a refuge of encouragement in our times of trial. It has been a source of nourishment in times of need. There have been so many times when not going to church or spending time with our friends would have been easy—and even logical. But it would have been a tragic mistake.

A man came to me years ago and offered me a job that could have paid me a fortune. He informed me that if I took the job I would have to spend evenings and weekends working. I told him that no amount of money would make me change my priorities from family and church and that I wasn't interested. He scoffed at me and all but called me a fool for turning down the job. Shortly after our conversation, his life and family fell apart. Mine didn't. I'm not better than him, but I was wiser than him in not allowing greed to pull me away from the foundation of Christian fellowship. In the parable of the sower, Jesus says these words to describe those who are overcome by the distractions of this life and forfeit their high calling to follow Him:

> "These are the ones sown among thorns; *they are* the ones who hear the word, and the cares of this world, the deceitfulness of riches, and the desires for other things entering in choke the word, and it becomes unfruitful" (Mark 4:18–19).

As believers in Christ, we must be grounded in church and Christian fellowship. I encourage you to break off unhealthy relationships. You don't have to be unkind or severe with those from whom you need to separate. In fact, you can share with them what the Lord has done in your life and invite them to join you in following Him. But you must be resolved not to remain in a spiritually compromising relationship with them.

Then you need to find a good "big church" and "little church." Be committed and don't give up. It may take a while but stay with it. Begin today. It is an essential step toward Christ and experiencing all that He has for you.

5

Knowing God through His Word

Your word *is* a lamp to my feet
And a light to my path.

—Psalm 119:105

When I received Christ, I didn't know anything about the Bible. I had heard sermons in which the Bible was quoted, but I didn't pay attention. When I was in the seventh grade, someone gave me a paperback copy of the New Testament called *Good News for Modern Man*. I put it in a drawer next to my bed but rarely read it. As I mentioned in the introduction, the main times I read it were evenings when I would come home drunk after a night of partying. So needless to say, when I received Christ, I didn't really know the Bible at all.

Shortly after I got saved, someone told me that I should start reading the Bible and that I should begin in the Gospel of John and the book of Psalms. That was good advice. Those are two books in the Bible that are easier to understand and that minister life to a newly born spirit.

I dedicated myself to reading the Bible, but I didn't really understand it much until I received the baptism of the Holy Spirit. The Holy Spirit inspired the writers of the Bible, and anytime you read it, you should rely on Him for understanding and guidance. Remember, He is the Spirit of Truth, and Jesus promised that He would guide us into all truth (John 16:13). The Bible is God's Word, the essence and standard of all truth.

Now that you are a believer in Christ, it is essential that you build a daily discipline in your life to read the Word of God. At the back of this book is a Daily Reading Guide that will help you read through the Bible every year. This is what I have done for many years, and I have found it to be very helpful. By reading just 15 or 20 minutes a day, you can learn the Bible as you allow the Word to minister to you and empower you to live for Christ.

All of what I have just stated can be summarized in one sentence: as a disciple of Jesus, you must know His Word, and to do this, you must discipline yourself daily to read it on your own. I cannot overstate the importance of this issue. Reading and knowing God's Word, the Bible, are essential in building a relationship with the Lord and learning how to live for Him.

What the Word Does for Us

Let me now explain what the Word of God does in our lives and why Bible reading is such a crucial practice:

*The Word of God renews our minds to think
as we should.*

> Do not be conformed to this world, but be transformed
> by the renewing of your mind, that you may prove what
> is that good and acceptable and perfect will of God
> (Romans 12:2).

Most of us understand that there are two essential
aspects working together to make computers do what they
do—hardware and software. The same is true of humans.
We have been equipped by God with incredible hardware:
namely, our brains. However, we have serious software
problems.

In the beginning, God programmed Adam and Eve with
His Word. Consequently, they were prepared to live for
Him and succeed in everything they did. Life was good ...
until a serpent slithered into the Garden of Eden one day
and spoke his first words to the human race: "Has God
indeed said, 'You shall not eat of every tree of the garden'?"
(Genesis 3:1).

Notice that the devil's first words to mankind were an
accusation against God and His Word. The devil knows
that he cannot defeat us until he disarms us. Therefore, his
incessant mission is to keep us ignorant of God's Word or, if
we happen to know it, to make sure we don't practice it.

Unfortunately, Adam and Eve succumbed to the devil's
deceptive skills, and a virus was downloaded onto their hard
drives. With faulty programming now controlling them, their
relationships with God and each other were ruined and their

destiny in God forfeited. They spread their virus to all their descendants, and the results were the chaos and destruction we see in the world today.

We must understand that we are born with the most advanced computer on earth sitting between our ears. It is truly amazing what God did in creating the human brain. What a gift! However, it doesn't matter how good the hardware is if it doesn't have the correct software. The Bible is the proprietary software from God that our hardware is designed to operate by so we can live successfully. It is so powerful that Psalm 1 promises we will succeed in everything we do if we meditate on God's Word day and night.

Meditating is simply the process of remembering God's Word and bringing it back into our minds to think upon. What a powerful promise that everything in our lives will succeed simply by loading the software of God's Word back into our minds and allowing it to continually guide us!

When we read the Bible, not only are we allowing God to reload the correct software into us, but it also has a virus removal program built into it. Read what the writer of Hebrews says about the remarkable power of God's Word:

> The word of God *is* living and powerful, and sharper than any two-edged sword, piercing even to the division of soul and spirit, and of joints and marrow, and is a discerner of the thoughts and intents of the heart (Hebrews 4:12).

You must understand this about the Bible: You read other books, but this book reads *you*! It is "living and powerful."

As you read the Word of God, it brings the light of God into you. As God's Word enters into your mind and spirit, it wars against every work of Satan that is in you. It is a "two-edged sword". It goes where no human being could ever go and does things no human force could ever do. It is the ultimate antivirus program that examines every thought and intent of the heart and removes those that are harmful.

When I look back on the way I thought 40 years ago compared to today, I am astounded. My life and mind have been transformed. I was set up for disaster as a young man because of the sin and deception deeply implanted in me. The power of God's Word has transformed me to think properly and has killed the viruses the devil downloaded to destroy me. This work still continues in me daily. It is amazing, and my life is successful because of it.

The Word of God creates intimacy with God.

> In the beginning was the Word, and the Word was with God, and the Word was God. He was in the beginning with God. All things were made through Him, and without Him nothing was made that was made. In Him was life, and the life was the light of men (John 1:1–4).

This text from John's Gospel is one of the most important in the Bible. It reveals Jesus as "the Word," who is God and the Creator of all things. Jesus is the perfect, living portrayal of the truth of God. His life is the embodiment of everything the Bible has to say. Thus, He is called "the Word."

Remember, the Bible isn't something; it is *someone*. We see this in another important verse:

> All Scripture *is* given by inspiration of God, and *is* profitable for doctrine, for reproof, for correction, for

instruction in righteousness, that the man of God may
be complete, thoroughly equipped for every good work
(2 Timothy 3:16–17).

The word "inspiration" literally means "God's breath" or
"breathed by God." In other words, all of the Bible is "God
breathed" and life-giving. It is Him! When we read it, we
aren't just learning something; we are experiencing someone—
God.

You will find that as you try to discipline yourself to
read the Bible, the devil will fight you tooth and nail. Why?
Because he knows that reading the Bible will cause you to
personally encounter and know Jesus. And the devil hates
Jesus and knows that once you are in relationship with
the Lord, his control over you is broken. I have found that
when I read the Bible, it always causes me to feel more alive
and spiritually strong than before I read it. But the most
important thing I have found in reading the Bible is that God
meets me there. He speaks to me, encourages me, loves me,
and comforts me. He becomes real through His Word, and my
personal relationship with Him grows in direct correlation to
my devotion to the Scriptures.

Here is what Jesus says concerning His words: "The words
that I speak to you are spirit, and *they* are life" (John 6:63).
This has been my experience in reading the Bible with a
reliance upon the Holy Spirit for guidance. It is life, and
through it I have a vibrant, intimate, and personal relationship with my Lord. It is simply not possible to know Him
apart from His Word.

The Word of God heals us.

> He sent His word and healed them,
> And delivered them from their destructions (Psalm 107:20).

When Karen and I got married, she had very low self-esteem. That really doesn't describe it accurately, though. She *hated* herself, and though she loved the Lord, she didn't think He loved her. Karen carried wounds from her childhood that had left her deeply scarred.

Karen is very physically attractive and always has been, but she believed she was ugly. Nothing I nor anyone else could say changed her mind. She constantly put herself down and doubted God's love for her. I have never met a person with more self-hate and lower self-esteem than Karen when we were first married.

In spite of her condition, she read the Bible every day. I literally haven't known a day since we married when Karen didn't read the Bible. When she first started reading it, she was confounded by it. She had an easy time believing the Scriptures about judgement and hell because they reinforced her belief that God didn't love her and wanted to punish her. However, when she read the Scriptures that spoke of God's love and mercy, she scoffed. She believed God loved others, but she couldn't receive it for herself.

I tried to console Karen and told her hundreds of times how beautiful she was and how much God loved her—but to no avail. However, she still woke up every day and read the Bible. It didn't happen overnight, but gradually the Word of God healed Karen and transformed her from a beaten-down girl into a lioness for God. Today, Karen knows God loves her, and she is a confident woman. No one but God can take the credit for it.

God also healed me through His Word. I had many issues in my life mentally, emotionally, and physically that were healed as I devoted myself to His Word. Let me give you an amazing example of this:

When Karen and I were first married, I began to develop small growths on my chin. I went to the dermatologist and had them removed. I did this over and over, and not only did they keep growing back, but they kept multiplying.

Finally, in a desperate attempt to be healed, I went to a specialist in Houston, Texas. After examining me, he told me that I would always have these growths and should just grow a beard to cover them. I was devastated. I left his office and wept in my car after hearing that news.

The next week, I was reading the Bible in my morning devotion time with the Lord that I refer to as a "quiet time." As I was reading, I came across this passage of Scripture:

> Jesus answered and said to them, "Have faith in God. For assuredly, I say to you, whoever says to this mountain, 'Be removed and be cast into the sea,' and does not doubt in his heart, but believes that those things he says will be done, he will have whatever he says. Therefore I say to you, whatever things you ask when you pray, believe that you receive *them*, and you will have *them*" (Mark 11:22–24).

As I read those verses, the Lord spoke to my heart and told me to speak to the growths on my chin and command them to be removed. The Word of God produces faith in us as we read it, and that is what it did for me that day (Romans 10:17).

The growths on my chin may have looked small to others, but to me they were mountains that were keeping me from God's best for my life.

If I hadn't been so desperate, I don't think I would have ever done it, but I walked into the bathroom, looked at myself in the mirror, and spoke these words: "In the name of Jesus, I command all of the growths on my face to leave now and never come back." I felt really foolish, but again, I was desperate. Nothing happened when I spoke those words, but I decided I was going to obey God until I saw results.

Every day for about 10 days, I spoke to those growths and commanded them to get off my face and never return. For many days nothing happened. But then one morning around the tenth day, I casually looked at myself in the mirror as I was about to brush my teeth. I noticed that all of the growths were completely gone. They had been there for years, and nothing had worked to get rid of them. But by the power of believing and confessing God's Word, I was healed and have never had another one again. Praise the Lord!

Here is what the book of Hebrews says about Jesus' role as our High Priest in heaven: "Holy brethren, partakers of the heavenly calling, consider the Apostle and High Priest of our confession, Christ Jesus" (Hebrews 3:1). Jesus is our Mediator and Advocate in heaven (1 Timothy 2:5; 1 John 2:1). He is there to intervene on our behalf and make sure we receive every blessing He died and rose again to give us. However, if you will notice in Hebrews 3:1, He is the Apostle and High Priest of our "confession." That means that the words of our mouths that are in agreement with God's Word enable Jesus to fulfill His ministry to us. Conversely, without a confession of faith, or because of a negative confession, we limit what Jesus can do for us.

You will notice in your own life and in the lives of others around you that we live at the level of our words. Part of the healing that God's Word ministers takes place within us as we read it and meditate upon it. But the rest takes place as we confess it over our lives, marriage, family, finances, and circumstances. The Word is powerful to heal, but we must put faith in it and let it direct our confession and change the nature of our speech.

The Word of God empowers us for victory over the devil.

> My brethren, be strong in the Lord and in the power of His might. Put on the whole armor of God, that you may be able to stand against the wiles of the devil. For we do not wrestle against flesh and blood, but against principalities, against powers, against the rulers of the darkness of this age, against spiritual *hosts* of wickedness in the heavenly *places*. Therefore take up the whole armor of God, that you may be able to withstand in the evil day, and having done all, to stand.
>
> Stand therefore, having girded your waist with truth, having put on the breastplate of righteousness, and having shod your feet with the preparation of the gospel of peace; above all, taking the shield of faith with which you will be able to quench all the fiery darts of the wicked one. And take the helmet of salvation, and the sword of the Spirit, which is the word of God. (Ephesians 6:10–17).

In this text, the apostle Paul makes it clear that our real enemy is in the invisible realm. So often we think that our biggest problems are with people we know, politicians of a different party, or even nations that are enemies to us. However, that isn't true. Before we get saved, our spirits are dead, and we cannot perceive the things of the Spirit or understand what is happening in the spiritual realm. Therefore, we are left to the physical realm, and we naturally try to deal with our issues and problems on that level.

However, now that we are saved and have received the fullness of the Holy Spirit, we can begin to understand the realities of the spirit realm. One of the most important realities we must be aware of is the presence of evil forces under the control of Satan that are sent to keep us from fulfilling God's will for our lives. Paul's exhortation to us in Ephesians 6 is to be aware of the presence of evil and to put on the armor that God has given us to defend ourselves and to overcome every attack of the enemy.

You see, even though there are enemies, we have been given authority over them to defeat them every time. This is what Jesus says about this issue: "Behold, I give you the authority to trample on serpents and scorpions, and over all the power of the enemy, and nothing shall by any means hurt you" (Luke 10:19).

Jesus has given us the ability to overcome every evil force that will ever come against us. He has defeated the devil for us and given us the birthright of victory. This is a huge blessing, one we must understand. However, we have to remember that the victory isn't automatic just because we are believers. We have to use the authority God has given us in order to succeed and live as we should.

Notice the sentence from Ephesians 6 that describes the Word of God as the sword of the Spirit. What a powerful picture! Also, notice that the Word of God is the only offensive weapon mentioned. Every other piece of armor is defensive against the "fiery darts" of the enemy. However, the Word is our sword and is able to strike a deathblow against every force that comes against us.

Nowhere is the reality of this truth more evident than in the battle between Jesus and Satan. Jesus was finishing His 40 days of fasting when the devil showed up to tempt Him. The entire battle between them was an exchange of words and thoughts. Here is how it went:

> Now when the tempter came to Him, he said, "If You are the Son of God, command that these stones become bread."
>
> But He answered and said, "It is written, 'Man shall not live by bread alone, but by every word that proceeds from the mouth of God.'"
>
> Then the devil took Him up into the holy city, set Him on the pinnacle of the temple, and said to Him, "If You are the Son of God, throw Yourself down. For it is written:
>
> 'He shall give His angels charge over you,'
> and,
> 'In *their* hands they shall bear you up,
> Lest you dash your foot against a stone.'"
>
> Jesus said to him, "It is written again, 'You shall not tempt the Lord your God.'"
>
> Again, the devil took Him up on an exceedingly high mountain, and showed Him all the kingdoms of the world and their glory. And he said to Him, "All these things I will give You if You will fall down and worship me."

> Then Jesus said to him, "Away with you, Satan! For it
> is written, 'You shall worship the Lord your God, and Him
> only you shall serve.'"
>
> Then the devil left Him, and behold, angels came and
> ministered to Him (Matthew 4:3–11).

Notice that in every case when the devil came with a half-truth or temptation, Jesus quoted the Bible to him: "It is written ..." The result was victory over the devil himself. We simply cannot understand the nuclear power of the Word of God in the realm of the spirit. It isn't just a sword; it is the most powerful weapon in the universe. One Scripture spoken by faith can vanquish the powers of hell.

For the rest of your life, you have an enemy in the devil and his minions, and they will try to defraud you of every blessing and promise God has for you. You will have to put on your armor and fight for victory. And God's Word is an essential part of your armor. With it you can win any battle. Remember the exhortation of the apostle Paul, "Be strong in the Lord and in the power of His might" (Ephesians 6:10).

The Word of God is God's power that works in us when we believe it and confess it. The devil will come to you with doubt, fear, condemnation, lies, confusion, deception, and temptation in order to defeat you. All you need to do is to find a Scripture that fits your circumstances and quote it to him, just as Jesus did.

For example, the devil may tell you that you will never succeed in life and that you are a loser. Maybe someone spoke those words over you earlier in life, and they created a wound that Satan is accessing. Don't accept his dark lies as defining who you are or what you can do. God's Word says something different for you: "I can do all things through Christ who strengthens me" (Philippians 4:13). As you put faith in God's Word for your life and begin confessing that you can do all things through Christ, it defeats the spirit of discouragement and fear the devil is attacking you with.

By the way, when the devil attacks, he doesn't announce himself. Remember, in the Garden of Eden he took the form of a serpent, and in Luke 10 (quoted earlier), Jesus says He gave us authority over "serpents." Serpents are stealthy. They are particularly dangerous because they blend into the environment.

The devil won't come to us announcing that he is present and wants to talk with us. No, he blends into our environment, silently introducing thoughts into our minds that he wants us to believe originated in our own minds or that even came from God. We must learn to uncover these negative and destructive thoughts and attribute them to their rightful source—the enemy.

As we uncover these thoughts, we can then defeat them by the power of God's Word. At the end of this book I have included a section that will show you where to find Scriptures you can use to overcome negative thoughts and circumstances you are currently encountering or might encounter in the future.

In Chapter 10, I will go into more detail about winning the battle for our minds. Specifically, I will teach you about the powerful practice of biblical meditation. You will find it to be your most important discipline for living in freedom and peace.

I hope you can see the importance of God's Word in your life. Along with your new daily discipline of reading and meditating on God's Word, you also need to be a committed part of a Bible-believing and Bible-preaching church. It is so important that you are being spiritually fed on a regular basis by a pastor who knows God's Word and can help you understand it. You can also join a small group or Bible study in your church that is studying a particular topic you are interested in. Whatever time and energy you invest in knowing God's Word will pay off eternally.

Congratulations! You have now taken your fifth step toward Christ. We are halfway through our journey together!

6

A Dynamic, Daily Prayer Life

Pray without ceasing.

—1 Thessalonians 5:17

What I love most about being a Christian is that it isn't about dead religious rituals or dogmas. It is a personal relationship with God. Nowhere is this more real than in prayer. I'm not talking about prayer that is obligatory and boring. I'm talking about a dynamic prayer life that bonds our hearts to God, nourishes our souls, and produces real results.

I so wish someone would have been with me when I became a believer to tell me how to pray. But no one was. All I knew was that I was supposed to pray. I took a class in church, and they instructed us that we were supposed to wake up early, read our Bibles, and pray. And so I dedicated myself to that practice.

But I had a really hard time with it. I fought sleepiness, boredom, and distraction by the moment. I had it in my mind that I was supposed to do this for one hour every morning. I think someone told me that. After

5 to 10 minutes, I had gone through my checklist of spiritual duties, and then came the hard part of trying to stay focused and awake. It was tough!

Today it is totally different. I wake up in the morning and enjoy rich times with the Lord. It is meaningful, engaging, and dynamic. I love it. In this chapter I am going to share with you some of the secrets I have learned about having a dynamic, daily prayer life. To do this, I am going to refer to the sixth chapter of Matthew's Gospel, where Jesus teaches us how to pray. The breakthrough in my prayer life came as I studied what He tells us about God and prayer.

Who God Really Is

I want to begin by focusing on an issue that you must understand if you are going to be successful in prayer: God loves you! He is your best Friend and your perfect Father. You see, we cannot get closer to God than our concept of Him will allow. If we believe He is distant and uncaring, it will be difficult for us to pray and have faith that He is listening. If we believe He is angry and against us, we will have a hard time getting motivated to pray.

Jesus' first major message in the Bible is the Sermon on the Mount. It is recorded in Matthew's Gospel beginning in chapter five. Then it continues in chapter six, where Jesus teaches us how to pray. What sets Jesus' teaching on prayer apart from all others is what He declares about God being our loving heavenly Father. Here is what Jesus says about this:

"Do not worry about your life, what you will eat or what you will drink; nor about your body, what you will put on. Is not life more than food and the body more than clothing? Look at the birds of the air, for they neither sow nor reap nor gather into barns; yet your heavenly Father feeds them. Are you not of more value than they? Which of you by worrying can add one cubit to his stature?

So why do you worry about clothing? Consider the lilies of the field, how they grow: they neither toil nor spin; and yet I say to you that even Solomon in all his glory was not arrayed like one of these. Now if God so clothes the grass of the field, which today is, and tomorrow is thrown into the oven, *will He* not much more *clothe* you, O you of little faith?

Therefore do not worry, saying, 'What shall we eat?' or 'What shall we drink?' or 'What shall we wear?' For after all these things the Gentiles seek. For your heavenly Father knows that you need all these things" (Matthew 6:25–32).

My first major obstacle in prayer had to do with my concept of God. I didn't *really* believe that He loved me—or knew me well, for that matter. I even thought at times that He was angry with me and wanted to punish me. So even though I loved Him and was trying to do the right thing as a Christian, I struggled because of a wrong concept of who God is.

Almost all of us develop our concept of God based on our parents, especially our earthly fathers. Our concept of God can also be based on spiritual leaders or other authority figures in our lives as we grow up. What our parents and key authority figures in our lives did, whether right or wrong, we naturally attribute to God. If they were loving and kind, we have a much easier time accepting God as a loving and gracious God. If they were absent or abusive, then we struggle to relate to God and believe He is truly concerned about us.

Parents are image bearers of God to their children, whether they realize it or not. This goes all the way back to the Garden of Eden when God created Adam and Eve, the original parents of the human race. God put His image on them first and then commanded them to be fruitful and multiply. Here is the account:

> So God created man in His *own* image; in the image of God He created him; male and female He created them. Then God blessed them, and God said to them, "Be fruitful and multiply; fill the earth and subdue it" (Genesis 1:27–28).

Adam and Eve were not ready to parent until they bore God's image. The reason is that the first role of parenting is to bring our children into a proper understanding of who God is. (By the way, this is also the first role of leadership in the church. As Christ's representatives, we are to demonstrate His character and nature to those we lead.)

Unfortunately, many parents don't understand that their role is to bear a true image of God to their children. But even if they do, all parents are imperfect. No parent bears a flawless image of God to his or her child. Therefore, all of us must come to a critical place in our spiritual lives that will set us free to grow in God and develop true faith and intimacy with Him. This is the place where we disassociate our parents' failures and flaws from who God is. This includes other authority figures who have wrongfully influenced our concept of God.

I want you to carefully think this through because it is so important to your spiritual future. Have you been hurt or disappointed by your parents? Were you abandoned by your father or mother? Were your parents absent, abusive, legalistic, and so on? I'm not trying to get you stirred up against your mom and dad—just the opposite. I want you to forgive your parents. I'll talk more about that a little later.

What I want you to see now is the direct correlation between your parents' behavior and your concept of who God is. Again, we cannot get closer to God than our concept of Him will allow. Our personal issues don't change who God really is. God is God, and He doesn't morph every time a child is wronged by his or her parents. He is immutable, which means He cannot change.

The Bible tells us who God is, and that is the truth we must hold onto, rather than allowing our past hurts to dictate how we relate to God. We must come to God and allow Him to reveal Himself as He really is. This is what Jesus did in Matthew 6. He was speaking to a multitude about prayer. In so doing, He taught them about a loving heavenly Father who knew them intimately and cared deeply about everything in their lives.

I struggled with my concept of God as a young Christian, but now I know I have a perfect Father who loves me and cares for me. Regardless of what your earthly parents were like, you need to rejoice that you now have a perfect Father. You are the apple of His eye, and you make His heart rejoice. He wants a close personal relationship with you, and He wants to care for you daily as His child.

Our Model Prayer

Now let's go to the next step in learning how to pray. Here is what Jesus says about the technique of prayer, commonly known as the Lord's Prayer. I heard this many times growing up but never understood it as an outline of how to pray. Once I understood that truth, it radically changed how I prayed. I have now prayed according to this model for more than 30 years.

Here is what Jesus says about how to pray:

> "But you, when you pray, go into your room, and when you have shut your door, pray to your Father who *is* in the secret *place*; and your Father who sees in secret will reward you openly. And when you pray, do not use vain repetitions as the heathen *do*. For they think that they will be heard for their many words.
>
> Therefore do not be like them. For your Father knows the things you have need of before you ask Him. In this manner, therefore, pray:

Our Father in heaven,
Hallowed be Your name.
Your kingdom come.
Your will be done
On earth as *it is* in heaven.
Give us this day our daily bread.
And forgive us our debts,
As we forgive our debtors.
And do not lead us into temptation,
But deliver us from the evil one.
For Yours is the kingdom and the power and the glory forever.
Amen.

For if you forgive men their trespasses, your heavenly
Father will also forgive you. But if you do not forgive men
their trespasses, neither will your Father forgive your
trespasses" (Matthew 6:6–15).

For the remainder of this chapter, we will go carefully
through this text to help you understand the importance of
what Jesus taught us about prayer. Once you understand this,
it will change your prayer life and, consequently, the rest of
your life too.

How to Pray

Let's begin with what Jesus says in the text just before He
teaches us the model of the Lord's Prayer. He gives two guide-
lines:

Pray privately.

First, Jesus tells us to pray in private. He says this because
the Jewish leaders of His day were prideful and prayed long
religious prayers on street corners to make themselves look
pious in the eyes of the people. They reduced prayer to an act
of public theater, having little to do with a personal relationship with God.

So our times of prayer with God should be in a solitary
place. This is really important. I know that it might not be
possible to find that private place in your home because of
children or some other reason. You might find your car in
the parking lot before work or school to be your best place

to pray. Any place will do as long as it provides you with the privacy you need. Some people even use closets in their homes as their sanctuary for prayer.

By the way, even though Jesus teaches us to pray alone, this doesn't mean we should never pray with other believers. There are many times when praying with other believers is essential to finding breakthrough for our personal lives or for a corporate need. However, this cannot be the basis of our prayer lives. A personal, daily time of prayer is essential to developing our relationship with God.

Pray succinctly.

Second, Jesus teaches that we should not use vain repetition. Again, the Jewish leaders of Jesus' day would ramble on and on about the same thing as they prayed, as though it made them look more spiritual, or as though God needed the nagging in order to get Him to act.

We must understand that prayer is speaking to God just like we speak to anyone else with whom we are in relationship. Of course, our relationship with God should be respectful, and it is on a different level than other relationships. But it is still a relationship in which we are speaking with God on a close, personal basis. You wouldn't say to your spouse, "Darling, Darling, Darling, Darling, Darling, Darling, Darling, Darling, Darling ..." It is really annoying and unnecessary. But I have known Christians who prayed like this: "Jesus, Jesus, Jesus, Jesus, Jesus, Jesus, Jesus, Jesus ..." I have heard people go on like this for several minutes. We need to know that God is with us and He hears what we say the first time.

What to Pray

Now we begin the Lord's Prayer. Remember, this is an outline of prayer, not just a prayer.

This is what many people (including me before I learned) don't understand concerning prayer. They read the text in Matthew 6 where Jesus teaches us to pray and conclude, *Well, that is a really short prayer. I guess all I need to do is say that prayer and I'm good.*

No, the Lord's Prayer is an outline. Every sentence of the prayer is a heading that allows us to pray particular prayers that belong there. When you use the model of the Lord's Prayer as your guide, you will find that when you are finished, you have completely unburdened your heart and have prayed for every area of your life. I use the Lord's Prayer as my model every day when I pray. I can pray for 10 minutes or two hours using the Lord's Prayer.

Let me go step by step to explain how to use it as your daily prayer guide.

Thanksgiving, praise, and worship

"Our Father in heaven,
Hallowed be Your name" (Matthew 6:9).

Your prayer time should always begin with thanksgiving, praise, and worship to God. "Father in heaven" is God's name and address. We are praying specifically to Him. We must focus our faith toward Him, as we believe He loves us and is listening to us. "Hallowed be Your Name" is both a prayer and a praise. The word *hallow* means "to sanctify, consecrate, or make holy." When we say this, we are actually saying three things:

"I worship You as a holy God."

We tell God that He is worthy of our worship and that we give Him the praise He alone deserves. This part of the prayer can last as long as you want it to. I would encourage you to spend at least four or five minutes at the beginning of your prayer time giving God thanks for all He has done for you, praising Him, and worshipping Him. It is the perfect way to begin. God loves worship, and the Bible says He is enthroned upon our praises (Psalm 22:3).

Thanksgiving, praise, and worship are crucial disciplines to keep our focus Godward. I can't say enough about the importance of this issue. You will find that the more you worship, the happier you are. The less you focus on yourself and your problems, the greater perspective you have on life and the closer you feel to God. Worship should be our default setting throughout our day.

"I set Your name apart in my life as sacred."

In other words, we say that we will not take His name in vain or use it disrespectfully.

"Show me who You really are, and show others who You are through me."

We should pray daily for God to reveal Himself to us in new ways and cause us to see Him without filters from our past or personality. "Hallowed be Your name" is a prayer for God to reveal Himself as He really is. I always accompany that part of the prayer with a request that God would use me to reveal His love and nature to others.

Surrender and direction

> "Your kingdom come.
> Your will be done
> On earth as *it is* in heaven" (Matthew 6:10).

The word *kingdom* means "direct rule." The kingdom of God is the realm of His rule. He is Lord. In this part of the prayer, we bring every aspect of our lives to God and surrender it to His will as we ask Him to guide and bless us.

Here is an example of how I pray in this area:

> Father, I surrender everything in my life to Your rule today, and I pray for You to reveal Your will to me. I need Your wisdom, guidance, and protection. I pray today that if I am doing anything apart from Your will, You would reveal it to me. Also, if there is any area of my life where I need to do something that I'm not doing, please reveal it to me and give me wisdom.
>
> Lord, today I am going to be having meetings with people, and I pray that You would guide every conversation. Give me discernment and wisdom. I surrender every area of these discussions to You and pray that only Your will would prevail at the end of the day.

As I pray, I go through my entire life and bring every decision, every anxiety, every relationship issue, and every personal issue in my life before Him. Prayer shouldn't be mundane or religious. It should be meaningful and dynamic. For this to happen, it means that you are speaking to God in prayer about what matters. In other words, what are you worrying about? Stop worrying and start praying! Your old worry list is your new prayer list. Who are you having problems with or need a better relationship with? Talk with God about them. What are your dreams or desires in life? Submit those to God and allow Him to partner with you in seeing your dreams come true.

God is your best Friend, and He knows you better than anyone else. You can't hide anything from Him. He's God! So don't pray with a closed heart. Come before God and tell Him everything you are going through, what you desire, and what you are worried about or are struggling with. Pray about sexual issues and temptations. Let God lead you to victory.

He knows what you're going through, and He cares about you. His throne is a throne of grace, and Jesus experienced all of our earthly temptations. With Him, we find grace and mercy for every issue in our lives (Hebrews 4:14–16).

Surrender your life to God, and you will find that He will do better for you than you will ever do for yourself. This is what I have discovered about Him. He loves me more than I love myself. I always thought God would take things from me if I ever truly surrendered. What I lost was the rubbish that was harming me. What I gained is beyond anything I ever dreamed. He is a good God.

Daily provision

"Give us this day our daily bread" (Matthew 6:11).

Notice that surrender comes before provision in the Lord's Prayer. This is an important point because God only blesses and provides for us when we are walking in His will. You need to understand this about God: His love is unconditional and cannot be earned. There is nothing you can do to make Him love you more or less. However, God's blessings are conditional on our obedience and faith in Him.

Once we are surrendered to God and walking in His will for our lives, He takes personal responsibility for us. As our Father, He provides, and He is the best provider in the world. He is generous, gracious, and faithful.

In this part of the prayer, you can bring all of your needs and desires to God. This includes financial provision, but it also means provision of friends, favor, jobs, promotions, houses, cars, help for our children, and much more. Anything you need is of concern to God. No issue is too large or too small.

When I have a need, I bring it to God every day until He provides. Then I praise Him for it when I receive it. I am constantly praising God for something else He has provided for me.

Forgiveness

"And forgive us our debts,
As we forgive our debtors" (Matthew 6:12).

Our God is an exceptionally gracious God. Jesus died for our sins so we can walk in an intimate, eternal relationship with God without our sins separating us from Him. As you get to know God better, you will find that He is very, very loving and gracious. He is the most kind and gracious person I have ever known.

But He is also holy. Therefore, we need to keep short accounts with God and ask Him to forgive us daily of those things that have stained our conscience before Him and have fallen short of His standards. As we confess these sins, God is faithful to forgive us and cleanse us spiritually (1 John 1:9).

We should be as detailed as we can be in this part of the prayer. If we forget something, God knows our heart and will certainly forgive us. But our attitude is important. If a person comes to this area of the prayer and just says, "Well, if I've done something wrong, please forgive me," that falls short of what God desires. Of course we've done things wrong. That is a no-brainer. We need to confess to God specifically what we did wrong and ask for forgiveness. This lets the Lord know that we take these things seriously and that we are walking in sincerity with Him. Once we have confessed and asked for forgiveness, we must accept by faith that we are forgiven. We don't have to feel bad for a number of days or punish ourselves.

Jesus died for our sins so we could be forgiven and receive the blessings of God we don't deserve. His part was to take our punishment. Our part is to repent and to walk before God in sincerity.

But we have another important part to play. We must forgive others who have sinned against us in order for God to forgive us. God will only give us as much grace as we will give away.

In Matthew 18:21–35, Peter asks Jesus if we should forgive a person seven times. Jesus responds that we must forgive seventy times seven. Jesus' meaning is that we must always forgive. He goes on to tell a story that I would encourage you to read for yourself. It is a warning about not forgiving others.

Forgiveness is an everyday issue between us and God and between us and others. We have a tendency to want justice for others and grace for ourselves. It doesn't work that way, though. You will be judged by God in the same manner and with the same standard that you judge others—grace for grace and justice for justice (Matthew 7:1–5). I don't know about you, but I want grace.

Forgive your parents, stepparents, spouse, ex-spouse, children, friends, enemies, boss, and anyone else in your past or present who you resent and are harboring ill will toward. I like this saying: "Forgiveness doesn't make them right; it just makes us free."

I will give you more detailed instructions about the three-step process of forgiving others in Chapter 9.

Guidance and protection

"And do not lead us into temptation,
But deliver us from the evil one" (Matthew 6:13a).

In this part of the prayer, we are praying for the Lord's continual guidance and protection. Again, when we are walking in God's will, we are walking under His protective covering. They go together. However, we can't run out the door every day doing our own thing and then ask the Lord for protection.

We must remember that we have an enemy—the evil one— who desires to steal, kill, and destroy our lives (John 10:10). Here is what the apostle Peter warns believers about the devil: "Be sober, be vigilant; because your adversary the devil walks about like a roaring lion, seeking whom he may devour" (1 Peter 5:8). We don't need to fear the devil, but we need to be aware that he lies in wait to harm us. As long as we are walking humbly with God and asking Him to direct and protect us, we are secure.

I have learned to respect God in this area a lot more than when I was young in the Lord. I am a motivated person, and I have a tendency to do things on my own and ask God to bless them later when I'm in distress. It has caused me a lot of heartache, and the Lord has taught me on more than one occasion that if I will slow down and walk with Him, things will be more peaceful, successful, and safe.

When I pray this part of the prayer, what I am doing is telling the Lord that I want to walk with Him today and that I don't want to sin or be tempted to sin. Of course, God would never tempt us, but He can lead us into a daily path away from temptation and harm. If we will humble ourselves and acknowledge His presence each day, He will be faithful to lead us into a blessed and protected path. We can also use this part of the prayer to pray protection for our spouse, children, loved ones, belongings, and so forth.

Acknowledgment of divine right

> "For Yours is the kingdom and the power and the glory forever. Amen" (Matthew 6:13b).

This part of the prayer is simple but profound. We must refuse for ourselves three things that human beings love to claim as their own: a kingdom, power, and glory. Jesus tells us to pray, "Yours is the kingdom and the power and the glory." "The" is a definite article. It refers to something specifically and solely. Notice that Jesus doesn't tell us to pray, "Yours is *a* kingdom and *a* power and *a* glory." "A" is an indefinite article, and it means there could be others.

God has the *only* true kingdom, the *only* real power, and the *only* right to glory. As we conclude our prayer time and set out to live for God, we must orient our hearts correctly. As I pray this part of the prayer each day, I remind myself that I don't have a kingdom, but I serve the kingdom of God. I don't have the power to live as I should, so I must rely on His power. And I don't deserve glory and should not seek it for myself. I live to bring Him glory, and He alone deserves it.

Saying "Amen" at the end of the prayer simply means "Let it be so." It's good to say, "In Jesus' name, Amen" when you pray because Jesus tells us that whatever we ask the Father in His name will be granted to us (John 15:16; 16:23). Praying in His name doesn't just mean that we say His name; it also means that our lives and the things we have prayed for are aligned with His purpose being fulfilled through us.

That's it! You've learned how to pray. Of course, there are other things you will learn as you grow in the Lord, but what you have learned in this chapter is the basis of how I pray every day and how Jesus taught us to pray.

I would encourage you to establish a time and place to pray every day. In my prayer times, I begin by writing in a journal. A spiral notebook can work great as a journal if you don't have anything else. I just write a page or so of my thoughts about life and the Lord. I have grown to really enjoy journaling.

Next, I use my daily reading guide to do my Scripture reading for the day. (There is a daily reading guide for you at the back of this book.)

I then pray using the Lord's Prayer as my guide. As I said before, I have done this for many years, and it is the foundation of my personal relationship with the Lord.

One area I didn't mention in this chapter is how to hear God speak to you. This is something that is very special about learning to how pray. Prayer isn't a monologue; it is a dialogue in which we speak to God and God speaks to us. I will address the issue of hearing God in Chapter 8.

Okay, four more steps to go. I hope you are feeling closer to Christ with every chapter. Let's keep going!

7

Stewardship

Let each one give as he purposes in his heart, not grudgingly or of necessity; for God loves a cheerful giver. And God is able to make all grace abound toward you, that you, always having all sufficiency in all things, may have an abundance for every good work.

—2 Corinthians 9:7–8

After Karen and I had been married for a couple of years, we moved to a community about 20 miles away from where we had lived all of our lives. When we moved, we started visiting churches that were closer to us.

One particular Sunday morning, we visited a church that adjoined a college campus. It had a young congregation, and we liked that. The pastor of the church seemed like a nice guy. That is, until he started preaching. On our first visit, he preached on giving money to the church. I hated it and knew right away I would never go back to that church again.

But I had a problem. Karen liked his message. When we got home, she told me that she agreed with his message and wanted to give 40 dollars to the church, if it was okay with me. I felt sick to my stomach. It was like an out-of-body experience. I just couldn't believe this was happening to me.

Forty dollars may not sound like a lot of money to some people, but our total income that year was seven thousand dollars. I made less than six hundred dollars a month, and we barely survived. When that preacher was talking about giving money to the church, I was thinking, *Buddy, I feel a lot sorrier for me than I do for this church. I think I'll just keep my money*!

But my wife didn't agree. In spite of our humble means, she asked me if she could give 40 dollars to the church. I had two thoughts swirling in my mind as she awaited my response. First, I thought to myself that if I said yes, we would go broke. We were on the edge of broke all the time, and that 40 dollars would surely push us over the edge. The other thought I had was that if I said no, God would strike me.

Something in my heart knew that giving was the right thing to do, but there was a major battle going on between my head and my heart. Finally, and in disgust, I told Karen to go ahead and give the money to the church. I just couldn't believe she had become that big of a fanatic.

What happened next surprised me.

Our Giving, the Lord's Blessing

I hope you can understand that I had no faith to give that 40 dollars, and I was skeptical about the entire concept of giving money to the church. It was my wife who got me into the whole mess. But actually, it wasn't a mess. It was one of the most important events in my life, and it has radically transformed my life ever since. Let me explain.

When Karen gave the money that week, I was sick and afraid. I just couldn't do the math. We never had enough money from paycheck to paycheck—never! The only way we made it was the "float" effect of being able to write checks and for them not to make it to the bank for a day or two until we got paid again.

So giving the 40 dollars was a big deal for us, and it was a lot of money to a struggling young couple with a baby. At that time I got paid every two weeks. What happened between the time we gave the money and the next time we got paid was remarkable. I didn't get a raise, and no extra money showed up. However, for the first time, we had some money in the bank the next time I got paid. It was a surprise and a huge relief.

Just as soon as I got comfortable with the fact that we weren't going to go broke and we had a little cushion in our checking account, Karen asked if she could give again. This triggered my gag reflex. I said something like "Karen, don't push it. We survived the last time, but why do you have to do it again?" She sweetly persisted until I relented and allowed her to give another 40 dollars. My mind raced with thoughts of living on the streets in a cardboard box as my pastor drove past us in the new car that our money had bought for him.

I had never before considered where churches get their money. The only time I had ever heard of giving money to the church was when they passed the offering plates during services when I was young. Even then, I never really thought about it. It was just a meaningless ritual to me. But now I had a crazy wife who was trying to bankrupt us by giving away our money to the church.

Or so I thought.

When Karen gave the second time, it was again remarkable what happened over the next two weeks. Once again, without a raise or any other source of income, we had extra money in the bank the next time I got paid. I started thinking that maybe God was doing something miraculous in our finances because of our giving. That was what our pastor said He would do if we gave. But at this point, I still didn't like the pastor. As far as I was concerned, he had talked my wife into doing something that almost drove us to the poorhouse. But now it was actually blessing us. Anyway, he was still a suspect, but I was keenly aware of a major difference in our finances.

But then, of course, my fanatical and overly generous wife asked if she could give again. This time I said yes without gagging, fainting, nagging, or having internal existential debates. So she gave again, and the positive financial trend continued. I finally remarked, "The Lord is blessing our finances because of our giving." (Notice I said "our" giving, as if I could take any credit for it!)

From that point forward, I became a partner with Karen in making sure that every time we got paid and had an increase financially, the first part went to the Lord.

Money's Link to the Heart

Again, I want to say that this issue has radically changed my life and the lives of thousands of others I have led into this experience as their pastor. I want to ask you to open your heart to the Lord as I help you understand the issue of stewardship and giving to the Lord. We are going to look at some important Scriptures that will help you understand this crucial issue and how it is inherently linked to our relationship with Christ.

That's right. How we deal with the issue of money and the overall issue of stewarding what God has entrusted to us is an issue of our hearts that cannot be separated from our relationship with Christ. Let me prove it to you by the words of Jesus Himself:

> "Do not lay up for yourselves treasures on earth, where moth and rust destroy and where thieves break in and steal; but lay up for yourselves treasures in heaven, where neither moth nor rust destroys and where thieves do not break in and steal. For where your treasure is, there your heart will be also" (Matthew 6:19–21).

In this passage of Scripture, Jesus doesn't forbid us to save money responsibly or plan for the future. Instead, He warns us about hoarding money as a source of security and focusing our lives on the here and now rather than on God. He tells us that we must lay up treasures for ourselves in heaven. The only way you can do this is by giving to the Lord. Whatever we give of our time, treasures, or talents in serving God and giving to our local church is eternalized in heaven.

But even more important than that is what Jesus says about our treasures being inseparably linked with our hearts. He tells us that wherever we put our treasures, that is where our hearts will be also. You cannot separate your treasures and your heart. Therefore, stewardship isn't primarily about money or God getting "our stuff." It is about our hearts and whether they will be focused on God or this world.

When I went to church and heard about giving for the first time, my heart was hardened to God in relation to money. I had lived on the edge of poor all my life, and I didn't want to be poor any longer. I had dreams of getting money and providing things for my family that I didn't have growing up. When that preacher started talking about giving money, it threatened everything I dreamed of, and it started a war in my heart that I would have lost if it had not been for my precious wife.

God didn't have my heart. Because my treasures weren't with God, my heart wasn't with Him either. He never has your heart until He has your treasures. They cannot be separated. Look at these words of Jesus from the same text we just read in Matthew's Gospel:

> "No one can serve two masters; for either he will hate the one and love the other, or else he will be loyal to the one and despise the other. You cannot serve God and mammon.
>
> Therefore I say to you, do not worry about your life, what you will eat or what you will drink; nor about your body, what you will put on. Is not life more than food and the body more than clothing? Look at the birds of the air, for they neither sow nor reap nor gather into barns; yet your heavenly Father feeds them. Are you not of more value than they?" (Matthew 6:24–26).

You see, money is about trust, and according to Jesus, we only have two choices—God or "mammon." Mammon simply means "the god of money and wealth." Jesus tells us that we can serve one or the other but not both.

Who are you going to serve? Or to put it another way, who are you going to trust? Jesus tells us that we can trust our Father in heaven with all of our needs, and He will provide for us faithfully. Giving and stewardship prove our trust in God and reveal where our hearts are.

This issue is so important that Jesus talked about it more than He did heaven or hell. One out of six verses in the Gospels are about money. And one-half of all Jesus' parables are about money and wealth. I pray you will not take this issue lightly or harden your heart as so many believers do when it comes to money. God wants to establish a relationship with you of intimate trust and dependence. He wants to bless you and provide for you in ways that you cannot imagine. But He cannot do those things when your trust is in money and not in Him.

As Karen and I began giving to the Lord, I saw God in a new way. I also began seeing money in a new and better way. Today, Karen and I give approximately 20 percent of our annual income to our local church and other ministries. We have the thrill of being able to give and know we are making a difference in people's lives. But we are also incredibly blessed ourselves. I haven't lost anything by giving to the Lord—just the opposite. I have seen His bountiful and miraculous provision year after year as I have grown in giving and stewardship. It is a deal with no losers.

My life has been blessed and transformed, and my relation-ship with God has grown immeasurably as I have seen Him reveal Himself over and over as my faithful Father and provider. I shudder when I think of what would have happened if I hadn't allowed Karen to give that first gift of 40 dollars and if my fearful, mistrustful heart had refused to allow God to reveal Himself to us.

I hope you can see how important this issue is in your relationship with Christ.

The Three Foundations of Stewardship

I now want to teach you the three basic foundations of stewardship so that you can understand this issue more fully.

We do not own anything.

> The earth *is* the Lord's, and all its fullness,
> The world and those who dwell therein (Psalm 24:1).

> "Whoever of you does not forsake all that he has cannot be My disciple" (Luke 14:33).

When Karen and I went to church and heard the message on giving that provoked my disgust and her generosity, the preacher quoted both of the verses above. He told us that we could not own anything and that everything belonged to God. I didn't like it. It bothered me.

He then shared this quote from the famous evangelist Billy Graham: "You cannot take anything with you when you die. I've never seen a hearse pulling a U-Haul." Others in the congregation laughed. I didn't. I thought to myself, *Well, maybe I'll be the first!*

It is true—not that I'll be the first, but that we don't own anything. Everything in our possession belongs to God, and He can repossess it at any time. We came into this world without anything, and we will leave the same way. And after leaving, we will stand in judgement before God and give an account for how we have stewarded (managed) what was His (Matthew 25:14–30; Hebrews 6:2).

There are several problems with living life as though we are the owners of what we have. First, it is a lie. Second, it causes us to control what we have and to put our trust in it rather than in God. Third, it causes us to keep it away from God and not allow Him to be Lord over everything. Fourth, it prevents God from blessing us and providing for us because we will not trust Him in that area of our lives.

Stewardship begins as we surrender everything to God's ownership and become His managers and servants. Remember, Jesus said we could serve either God or mammon. Serving mammon is serving a false god. Serving God is true worship, and it means we are living our life in truth. We cannot own, but we can enjoy a life of incredible blessing as God's stewards.

The first belongs to God.

> Honor the Lord with your possessions,
> And with the firstfruits of all your increase;
> So your barns will be filled with plenty,
> And your vats will overflow with new wine (Proverbs 3:9–10).

> "Seek first the kingdom of God and His righteousness, and
> all these things shall be added to you" (Matthew 6:33).

God must be first in our lives in real terms. The first commandment God gave to the children of Israel through Moses was "You shall have no other gods before Me" (Exodus 20:3). Anything we put before God is an idol and a false god. That is the truth.

The other truth is that God deserves first place in our lives. He is awesome and good, and no other person, pursuit, or possession belongs in His place. Giving and stewardship prove who or what is first in our lives. And this issue isn't just about money. It is about every area of our lives. That is why I included both the passage from Proverbs and the one from Matthew. Proverbs 3:9–10 speaks of the first of our wealth and financial increase going to God, and Matthew 6:33 speaks of our time, energy, and talents being given to God first.

True stewardship means giving the first of our time, talents, and treasures to God. I hope you paid attention to the promises given in those verses. They are awesome, and they are true. As we give our first and best to God, He promises His best in return. I can assure you that He means it. We will never out-give God. Never. Every time we give, it provokes His blessings in return.

The life of stewardship is the most exciting and blessed way to live your life. I have heard miracle stories for more than 30 years as individuals and couples have taken the step of becoming stewards and giving the first of their lives to God. I have seen people go from poverty, bankruptcy, and hopelessness to blessing and prosperity as they took the faith step of stewardship and trusted God.

As a steward, you can know that your heart will stay connected to God. Remember, your treasures and your heart will always stay in the same place. Giving God the first of your time means giving Him the first day of the week, Sunday. (By the way, Sunday can begin Saturday evening. In the Bible, days begin at evening, not morning. See Genesis 1:5.) Giving God the first of your time also means giving Him the first of your day to pray and seek Him. Some people are not morning people, so if you're one of them, just give Him your best time of the day. Giving God the first of our talents means that we serve the Lord by using our gifts and abilities to serve our local church and those in need. We can do this by volunteering in the nursery at church, in children's or youth ministry, in choir, in worship, in teaching, in a mercy ministry or soup kitchen, or in many other areas. It is just important that we are contributing to God's work through our gifts and abilities on a committed and regular basis. Without serving, we naturally become selfish and distracted from the Lord.

If we don't serve, then we are also wasting the abilities God has given us. Preachers and church staff aren't the only gifted ones. Every believer is gifted and called to serve the Lord.

Giving God the first of our money means giving tithes and offerings. The word *tithe* means "10 percent." Giving begins by returning the first 10 percent of our income to the Lord. Everything after that is called "offerings." This is an important Scripture text about tithes and offerings:

"Will a man rob God?
Yet you have robbed Me!
But you say,
'In what way have we robbed You?'
In tithes and offerings.
You are cursed with a curse,
For you have robbed Me,
Even this whole nation.
Bring all the tithes into the storehouse,
That there may be food in My house,
And try Me now in this,"
Says the Lord of hosts,
"If I will not open for you the windows of heaven
And pour out for you *such* blessing
That *there will* not *be room* enough *to receive it.*
"And I will rebuke the devourer for your sakes,
So that he will not destroy the fruit of your ground,
Nor shall the vine fail to bear fruit for you in the field,"
Says the Lord of hosts (Malachi 3:8–11).

Most people freak out when they hear they are supposed to give 10 percent of their income to the Lord. I did! (By the way, I believe the first 10 percent comes from the gross income, before taxes and other deductions.) Your mind may be reeling right now with thoughts like *I just can't do that! There is no way. I'm already broke. That will ruin me.* I can totally identify with all of those thoughts. But they are wrong.

The passage from Malachi is God making His argument to Israel concerning their rebellion against Him. He has several issues with their condition, but one of the main ones is their refusal to give. God calls it robbery. You see, we don't *give* a tithe; we *pay* a tithe. The first belongs to God. You don't start giving until after the first 10 percent. That is when it becomes an offering.

I want to encourage you not to think about the dollars involved for just a minute and look at what God says in Malachi 3. First of all, He tells Israel they are cursed because of their refusal to give. This means it doesn't matter how much money they have or try to get; He will not allow it to prosper. He is working against them because they are going the wrong way, and He is trying to turn them around.

Second, God tells them that He has the ability to "rebuke the devourer" for their sakes if they will return to Him by giving tithes and offerings obediently. The devourer is God's collection agency. You see, you will never keep a tithe from God. When you don't give it, He will collect it one way or the other. You will give it to God, or you will give it to the auto mechanic, the appliance store, the doctor, the plumber, or someone else who has to fix your unblessed life and the things in it. By the way, giving doesn't ensure you'll never have problems, but it radically reduces the negative and increases the positive.

God also promises in Malachi that if we will give obediently, He will open the windows of heaven and pour out a blessing too great to receive. This is what Karen and I have experienced. God says we can test Him in this. It is the only area of our lives where we are allowed to test God. This means we can have a little attitude when we give our first tithe, like "Okay, God. I'm doing my part. Now let's see if You are real and if You are going to do what You said You would do." We are only allowed to have this attitude related to giving.

I challenge you to test God in this. It may be the scariest thing you've ever done, but it will change your life—and God will meet the test! He isn't limited. He can turn your mess into a miracle, but it won't happen until you give. I like this saying: "God can turn your little into much, but He won't turn your nothing into something."

Incidentally, tithes should go to your local church, "the storehouse." Give 10 percent of your income faithfully to your local church, and not only will you get the blessing of giving but you will also see God move powerfully in your finances.

As you become obedient in tithing, then you can also give offerings to other ministries and opportunities as God directs you.

Stewardship begins by surrendering our lives to God.

> I bear witness that according to *their* ability, yes, and beyond *their* ability, *they were* freely willing, imploring us with much urgency that we would receive the gift and the fellowship of the ministering to the saints. And not *only* as we had hoped, but they first gave themselves to the Lord, and *then* to us by the will of God (2 Corinthians 8:3–5).

The apostle Paul wrote this portion of Scripture concerning the churches in the area of Macedonia and how they gave generously to an offering he was collecting for the saints in Jerusalem. Paul uses their incredible generosity as an example as he asks the church at Corinth to also take part in the cause.

In referring to the generosity of the Macedonians, Paul reveals the secret of their abundant giving: "They first gave themselves to the Lord." Successful stewardship simply cannot happen until we surrender our lives to God. This is what He is after. Money, time, talents, or anything else we may give to God aren't really the focus of stewardship. It is a partnership between God and us that includes our entire lives.

Once God has us, He has everything we have. When God doesn't have us, nothing else we have can take our place. We can't put an offering in the plate on Sunday as a replacement for ourselves. No, our giving is a representation of the fact that we are completely given to God.

God has a purpose for your life. He made you in your mother's womb, and He is the only one who knows who you really are and what your true purpose in life is (Psalm 139). It is a sad thing to see so many people in the world waking up every day not knowing why they exist. They go through the motions of working, making money, paying bills, and getting by another month, just to start the same old cycle all over again. But your life is about so much more. Not only can you live your life with financial and personal blessing, but you can also live knowing that you are fulfilling God's higher purpose. It all begins by surrendering to God and committing everything you have to serving Him and furthering His kingdom.

Stewardship links our hearts and our lives in a practical, dependent, daily walk with the Lord. Without stewardship, we will always struggle and wander in our faith. There will always be a tension and incongruity between what we profess and what we live.

But when we are stewards, it means our treasures and our hearts are with God. We have refused the false god of mammon for the true and living God. Our lives are yielded to

God and His higher purpose, and we live a blessed life with the Lord as our faithful provider.

That was a big step! But you did it. I'm proud of you. Let's keep going.

8

Hearing God

"My sheep hear My voice, and I know them, and they follow
Me. And I give them eternal life, and they shall never perish;
neither shall anyone snatch them out of My hand."

—John 10:27–28

You cannot develop a relationship without communication that goes both ways. Not only does God want us to pray to Him and keep an open line of daily communication, but He also speaks to us in a regular manner as our Shepherd and Lord. This is what makes Christianity a relationship with God and not a dead religion.

Over the years, I've heard some Christian leaders say that God doesn't speak anymore. I always think two things when I hear that. First of all, do they read the Bible? Second, if they are right, I must be out of my mind because I have been hearing a voice guiding me since I was born again in 1973, and that voice has been consistent, loving, scriptural, and 100 percent accurate.

Thankfully, those who scoff at God and don't believe He speaks to us are not correct. Not only does the Bible tell us very clearly that God speaks, but it is the common experience of millions of Christians throughout the ages.

In my case, on the first day I was born again, God spoke to me and told me never to see my friends again. Two weeks later, the Lord spoke to me when He called me into the ministry. I have now heard the Lord speak to me hundreds of times about many different issues.

Just as Jesus said, "My sheep hear My voice," I am so thankful that He speaks to us. I have told the Lord many times in prayer that I cherish His words to me. I truly do. I consider God's voice to be one of the most important treasures in my life. I have made every important decision in my life on what He has spoken to Karen and me. I have no regrets.

Now I want to teach you about the basics of hearing God. God loves you, and as your Shepherd, He wants to lead you in a personal and relational manner. He does this by speaking to you. This is a huge issue because it is the key to a dynamic, personal relationship with God. It is also the key to living your life successfully as you make your decisions based on God's voice guiding you. What an incredible blessing we have in being able to get direction, comfort, and loving correction directly from the Lord Himself!

Common Hindrances to Hearing God

In teaching you how to hear God, I first of all want to help you understand what hinders us from hearing Him. Even though God speaks, many believers don't hear His voice because of certain issues in their lives. Here are some of the main hindrances to hearing God.

Unconfessed sin

> Behold, the Lord's hand is not shortened,
> That it cannot save;
> Nor His ear heavy,
> That it cannot hear.
> But your iniquities have separated you from your God;
> And your sins have hidden *His* face from you,
> So that He will not hear.
> For your hands are defiled with blood,
> And your fingers with iniquity;
> Your lips have spoken lies,
> Your tongue has muttered perversity (Isaiah 59:1–3).

If you are married, you can understand what it is like to have offended your spouse by saying or doing something wrong. You try to carry on a conversation, and you notice he or she isn't speaking to you. As you press in to figure out what the problem is, you find that you hurt your spouse's feelings, and he or she isn't over it. Until you make it right, there simply isn't going to be conversation as normal.

The same is true of the Lord but on a different level. We don't have to be perfect for God to speak to us. He is a very gracious God. However, there are things that violate Him and keep Him from speaking to us until they are made right. One of them is the sin of unforgiveness. Another is immorality. Also, vulgar and hateful speech can offend God and hinder Him from speaking to us until we make it right.

As we pray daily, it is important for us to confess our sins and be sensitive to the Lord for any area He convicts us about.

As we confess our sins, He forgives us, and our relationship is completely restored. God doesn't sulk or browbeat us after we've repented. You will find Him to be the most gracious and faithful Friend you've ever had.

Rebellion

A man recently told me that the Lord hadn't spoken to him in a long time.

I asked him, "How long has it been since God spoke to you?"

"About a year," he replied.

"And what did the Lord say the last time He spoke to you?"

He didn't even hesitate to tell me. "He told me to confess to my wife that I cheated on her."

I was taken aback for just a moment. Then I asked, "And did you?"

"No."

After this, I had a lot of things to say to him. One thing I made sure he heard was this: "God isn't going to speak to you again until you've obeyed the last thing He told you to do."

Sadly, this man is far from being alone. A lot of people treat God's voice as though it were just another person speaking. They think they can listen and then decide whether to obey or not, depending on what God said. If this is your concept of God's voice, you aren't going to be hearing much from Him.

God is God. He is our Lord, and when He tells us something, He expects us to obey. When we refuse, He stops speaking. He still loves us and still desires a relationship with us. However, He won't tolerate disrespect and rebellion. We must obey Him when He speaks and let Him know we cherish His voice.

When we don't obey, we must take responsibility for our behavior and repent before He will speak to us again.

Busyness and distraction

In Chapter 6 I told you about the importance of prayer and how it establishes a dynamic personal relationship between the Lord and us. I also showed you the text of Scripture from Matthew 6 where Jesus tells us to pray in private.

All of us must discipline ourselves to find a quiet, private place to pray and hear God every day. Ninety percent of everything I've ever heard God say to me was in my "quiet time." That is what I refer to as my prayer and devotion time with the Lord. I have found that it is much easier to hear God when I am by myself as I stop to pray and listen to Him. Even though God can speak in any situation, He doesn't speak nearly as much in the busy circumstances in our lives. In other words, God isn't obligated to chase us down and tell us what we need to know. We are obligated to stop and hear Him.

We don't have time not to pray. We may think we are too busy, but when we pray, it breaks the tyranny of urgency over our lives and puts our priorities where they should be. Also, when we put God first and slow down to hear Him, He speaks—and one word from Him can change our lives. His voice makes us wiser than our enemies and gives us the keys for victory in every area. Again—we don't have time not to pray.

Those three things are the main problems that keep God from speaking to us. If you can relate to any of them, I encourage you to pray and make it right with God. He will forgive you, and you will then be prepared to hear Him.

Five Ways God Speaks to Us

Once we are ready to hear God, we then need to know how God speaks and how to recognize His voice. For the remainder of this chapter, I will teach you the five main ways God speaks to us and how to recognize His voice in our lives.

Through His still, small voice inside our hearts

> Behold, the Lord passed by, and a great and strong wind tore into the mountains and broke the rocks in pieces before the Lord, *but* the Lord *was* not in the wind; and after the wind an earthquake, *but* the Lord *was* not in the earthquake; and after the earthquake a fire, *but* the Lord *was* not in the fire; and after the fire a still small voice (1 Kings 19:11–12).

In 1 Kings 19, the prophet Elijah encounters God through a "still, small" voice. This is the best way to describe God's voice in our lives. God's voice is profoundly audible, though it isn't distinguishable by our physical ears.

Someone asked me once why God speaks with such a still, small voice in our hearts. I gave him a twofold answer.

First, God doesn't have to speak loudly because He lives in our hearts. When someone is standing right beside you, he doesn't need to speak loudly. Also, if he is standing right beside you and speaks too loudly, you can't hear him clearly. Volume becomes a liability.

The second reason God doesn't speak loudly is because He doesn't want to intimidate us. If God were to bark His commands in our hearts, we could easily get the idea that He is austere and non-relational. It is the quite opposite. He is gentle and loving. He wants an intimate, personal relationship and speaks to us on those terms.

One other thing: God doesn't have to speak loudly in order to be heard. God is a master of communication, and He speaks our language. He knows just how to speak to all of us. As you begin to hear God, you will find that His voice is crystal clear, though it is still and small.

I encourage you to ask God to speak to you. Then get quiet and listen. He will begin to speak to you.

Some might say, "Well, how do I know I'm not speaking to myself or it isn't the devil trying to deceive me?" That is a good question, and I've got a couple of responses.

First of all, we speak to ourselves all day, every day. It shouldn't be hard to distinguish our own voice.

Second, concerning the devil, he is pretty easy to spot because he will always end up saying something that disagrees with Scripture. Also, he uses condemnation and fear to try to intimidate us. God never does that.

When you are hearing from God, it is loving, consistent, and always scriptural. The most important thing to do as you begin to hear God's voice is to follow it. If the Lord tells you to turn to a Scripture, turn there. If He tells you to do something, do it. The more you respond to God's voice, the more He will speak and the more you will learn to recognize Him.

On the day I got saved, the Lord spoke to me and told me never to see my friends again. It wasn't what I would have done naturally. That is how I know it wasn't my voice. Also, it was an important step in my breaking away from sin and living for Christ. That is how I know it wasn't the devil's voice. It was also consistent with Scripture and has borne good fruit for many years. That is how I know it was God's voice.

As you pray and ask God to hear you, listen for a still, small voice inside your heart that is the most loving voice you've ever heard. That is God. Follow that voice!

Through the rhema word of God

> Faith *comes* by hearing, and hearing by the word of God (Romans 10:17).

In the Scripture above, "word" is the Greek word *rhema.* It means "the living voice of God" or "the now word of God." The Apostle Paul tells us in this Scripture that faith is born in us when God's Word comes alive to us, and He speaks it to us in a personal manner.

As you read your Bible daily, you give God an opportunity to speak a *rhema* word to you. He does this as you read the *Logos,* which is the written Word of God. People who don't read their Bibles are missing an opportunity for God to speak to them and build their faith.

As I have woken up in the mornings and read my Bible through the years, I have had hundreds of experiences where I was reading along, and then, all of a sudden, a Scripture would jump off the page at me. God used it to speak a *rhema* word that brought light and life into my heart as it also built my faith in that area.

Just last week, as I read a passage I had read many times before, the Lord highlighted a Scripture and used it to bring loving correction to me in an area of my life. Even though it was corrective, it was life-giving and very loving.

Many times the Lord speaks to us directly. But other times, He will only speak to us through His written Word. Of course, everything in the Bible is God speaking to us. But I am referring to those times when God is speaking a "now word" to us for a specific reason. God wants us to know the Bible and be devoted to it. We should read the Bible for many reasons, as I stated in Chapter 5, but also because He uses it powerfully at times as a means for His "living voice" to speak into an area in our lives where we need it at that time.

As you sit down to read the Word daily, ask the Holy Spirit to help you understand it. Also, ask God to give you a *rhema* word as you read. You will find that He will do it often, and those nuggets of truth will transform your life as you receive and obey them.

Through a sense of peace

> Let the peace of God rule in your hearts, to which also you were called in one body; and be thankful (Colossians 3:15).

The apostle Paul tells us in this Scripture to let the peace of God "rule" in our hearts. The word "rule" in this verse is the Greek word *brabeuo*. It means "to umpire; to decide." The peace of God in our hearts is one of the most important ways that God speaks to us daily. Through His peace, He guides us situationally, just as an umpire directs a game situation by situation.

Many decisions we make in life aren't in the Bible. Even though there are principles in the Bible that we should always obey, many decisions in life just aren't specifically mentioned. These include: Which major should I choose in college? Which job should I take? Where should I go to church? Which house should I buy? Where should I send my children to school?

These, plus hundreds of other decisions we make, aren't found specifically in the Bible. As we pray for direction from the Lord, in many cases He doesn't answer by saying something to us—He answers through His peace.

Here is what Jesus says concerning the guidance of His peace:

> "The Helper, the Holy Spirit, whom the Father will send in My name, He will teach you all things, and bring to your remembrance all things that I said to you. Peace I leave with you, My peace I give to you; not as the world gives do I give to you. Let not your heart be troubled, neither let it be afraid" (John 14:26–27).

As Jesus informs His disciples and us that He is sending His Holy Spirit to teach us all things, He then reveals that His peace will accompany the presence of the Holy Spirit in His mission to guide us. Jesus also tells us that His peace isn't like the peace that the world gives.

You see, the world's peace is external, fragile, and circumstantial. It can't be trusted. On the other hand, God's peace is eternal, enduring, and beyond your circumstances. God's peace is truly profound, and it is tangible. You can literally feel the peace of God when it is guiding you.

As you seek the Lord for His guidance, you should always pay attention to the level of peace in your life regarding the issue you are seeking Him about. There will be times in your life when everything in the natural looks right, but you just don't feel peace about it. That is God telling you no. Pay attention when you don't have peace. It is God speaking to you.

There will be other times when everything around you is falling apart and seems impossible, but for some reason you feel peace about it. That is God telling you yes. Remember, we walk by faith and not by sight (2 Corinthians 5:7). God has an eternal perspective and isn't limited by circumstances. That is the wonderful thing about being led by God. He knows what is around every corner, what is in every person's heart, and what is going to happen tomorrow. You can trust Him!

Karen and I have a policy regarding all of our decisions. We always make our decisions together. It is one of the most important factors in a good marriage. So many times when we are making important decisions, we do so based on peace. Just the other day we were praying about something, and Karen told me, "Jimmy, I just can't get peace about it."

We don't act unless both of us have peace. When Karen told me she didn't have peace, I respected it. Because of her feeling, we said no to that decision. We have never made a mistake with a decision when we followed God's peace. But many times when we were young in the Lord, we weren't sensitive and obedient when God withdrew His peace, and we always regretted those decisions.

Peace is one of the precious possessions we as believers have as a free gift from the Lord. Many people today who are addicted to drugs, alcohol, sex, and other things are simply seeking what God offers to all who will follow Him. As you pray daily for direction, don't forget God's peace. It will follow you throughout the day and "umpire" those decisions that can come at us so fast. It is an important way God speaks to us.

Through open and closed doors

"And to the angel of the church in Philadelphia write,

'These things says He who is holy, He who is true, *He who has the key of David, He who opens and no one shuts, and shuts and no one opens*'" (Revelation 3:7 emphasis added).

There are many times in life when we pray for direction and God uses circumstances to tell us what He is saying. I call this guidance through "open and closed doors."

There have been times in my life when I have become frustrated with God because a door of opportunity would not open for me—or even got slammed in my face. When I look back, though, I can see the sovereign guidance of God in my life through open and closed doors. In fact, I now find it precious and heartwarming.

We don't realize how doting God is over us. He knows His purpose and destiny for us, and He doesn't want us to get off track. Also, as our heavenly Father, He is protective and doesn't want us to be harmed. Therefore, He uses circumstances to open doors for us and close doors to us.

Now, it isn't the only way He speaks. And just because a door of opportunity is opened or closed, that doesn't necessarily mean God is speaking. We have to be sensitive to Him and allow Him to interpret it for us. In some cases, when a door is closed, it doesn't mean God is saying no. It might be that He is saying, "Not now." In other cases, when an opportunity is open to us, it might be that God will not give us peace to walk through it. Again, it may not be a permanent no, but it might be a timing issue.

Here is a prayer that I pray often: "Lord, open doors for me that no man can close, and close doors for me that no man can open until I am standing in Your perfect will for my life." He answers such a prayer. In praying it, I align my heart with God's sovereign will, and as a result, I become much more sensitive to His guidance.

Don't be discouraged when a door is closed. There will be another one open to guide you into God's will for your life. He is faithful and is working all around you to guide and keep you.

Through other people

God often uses people to speak to us. In fact, there are things He will say to us only through others.

One of the primary people He uses is a wife or husband. I can't count the times that God has spoken to me through Karen or to Karen through me. God wants to remind us that we need each other. He also wants us to be humble and teachable in our relations with others. This is most true in our marriages.

God also uses parents to speak to children. This is obvious. But even though as adults we aren't under our parents' authority, God can still use them to speak to us. An example is Jesus. At the age of 12, He wanted to stay in Jerusalem and be about His Father's business. His mother, Mary, told Him no and took Him home. Jesus respected her authority and listened to her (Luke 2:41–51).

When Jesus was 30, He and His mother attended a wedding at Cana of Galilee. At the wedding the host ran out of wine. Mary turned to Jesus for a solution. Surely she had already witnessed His miraculous powers, even though His public ministry had not yet begun. Jesus was put out when Mary turned to Him. He even told her that His time had not yet come. However, He obeyed her, and that was the beginning of His public ministry (John 2:1–11). God used Mary to speak to Jesus when He was a child and an adult.

God also uses authority figures to speak to us. He even uses those who are unsaved and unfair. Here is what the book of Romans tells us about authority:

> Let every soul be subject to the governing authorities. For there is no authority except from God, and the authorities that exist are appointed by God. Therefore whoever resists the authority resists the ordinance of God, and those who resist will bring judgment on themselves. For rulers are not a terror to good works, but to evil. Do you want to be unafraid of the authority? Do what is good, and you will have praise from the same. For he is God's minister to you for good (Romans 13:1–4).

One of the things we need to understand about God's kingdom is that it is one of authority and structure. The devil's kingdom is one of chaos and rebellion. God will never lead us to rebel against authority. Even if those in authority are evil and we have to refuse obedience for conscience's sake because they are asking us to sin, we still must do it with a respectful and careful attitude. God respects authority and wants us to also.

God also uses church authority, counselors, consultants, fellow believers, friends, and others to speak to us at times. As you pray for guidance, be sure to listen to the voices of others around you. You obviously can't listen to everyone because they aren't saying the same thing. But you can listen for those times when someone is saying something to you that God confirms in your heart is from Him. This is especially true of our spouses and those in authority over us.

God speaks to us today. It is the basis of our personal relationship with Him and His personal guidance in our lives. Seek God daily in His Word and through prayer. As you do, ask Him to speak to you as you examine your heart and keep it pure before Him. Be sensitive to His voice in the five areas we have discussed. It won't take you long to begin to hear Him and personally witness the difference it makes in your life.

This is an important step toward a dynamic, personal relationship with the Lord. You are doing so well.

The next step is also very important.

9

Freedom from Your Past

Stand fast ... in the liberty by which Christ has made us free,
and do not be entangled again with a yoke of bondage.

—Galatians 5:1

When we are born again and filled with the Holy Spirit, our lives become radically different. We are now headed toward heaven with Christ in our hearts. Our purpose for life is transformed as we make the decision to follow Christ. Yet as we commit our future to the Lord, there is still some important housekeeping from our past that we must take care of.

Almost all of us have things in our past that, if we don't deal with them properly, will compromise our ability to live for God. In fact, I believe every person has issues from his or her past that must be dealt with. I did, and I waited too long to deal with them.

When I received Christ, I had no idea that I should deal with my past. It was years before anyone taught me what I will teach you in this chapter. When I learned about dealing with my past, it changed my life and set me free to live for

Christ in a greater manner. Also, because I hadn't dealt with issues from my past, I was carrying baggage that compromised every relationship and endeavor in my life. I didn't realize how big a problem it had become until it was removed.

I wrote another book called *Freedom From Your Past*. It chronicles my journey to freedom, and in it I, along with my coauthor, Ann Billington, describe how to be set free from every issue in your past. It goes into much more depth than I will in this chapter.

Here, though, I will talk about the three most important issues from our past that must be dealt with properly before we are free to go forward with the Lord. They are unforgiveness, iniquities, and inner vows.

Three Steps to Achieving Freedom from Unforgiveness

Unforgiveness is like an invisible umbilical cord that connects us to those we haven't forgiven. The event that caused us to harbor ill will toward them may have occurred 20 or 30 years ago, but until we forgive them, we are still connected. They may even be dead, but our lack of forgiveness keeps the umbilical cord connected and keeps feeding our spirits with poison from our past.

The worst problem with unforgiveness is that it blocks God's grace from flowing into our lives. As Jesus clearly teaches us, when we will not forgive others, God will not forgive us (Matthew 6:14–15). He will only give us grace and mercy to the degree that we give it away. You will always notice that when you accumulate grievances toward others, your relationship with the Lord suffers.

In Matthew 6, Jesus teaches us to daily ask God's forgiveness as we forgive those who have sinned against us. It needs to be a daily prayer because it is a daily occurrence. People are regularly doing things that hurt and upset us. It is also easy to pick up offenses on behalf of those we love.

Besides those things happening daily, most of us have endured some deep hurts in our past that naturally produce bitterness and unforgiveness if we don't deal with them properly. Issues like abuse, abandonment, neglect, rejection, divorce, infidelity, theft, and betrayal are common things that cause deep hurts that produce unforgiveness.

We are not free until these issues are resolved. First of all, we aren't free because God knows we haven't forgiven the people involved, and He won't lead us forward as we desire until we have obeyed Him in the crucial area of forgiving others. For example, most people need to forgive their parents. It is a big deal with God how we treat our parents. Regardless of what they have or have not done, we must forgive them to go forward with the Lord.

In addition, when we haven't forgiven, we aren't free because the bitterness from unforgiveness changes our personalities and keeps God from loving others through us. Bitterness toward people in our past causes us to be hard, harsh, mistrustful, rude, overly sensitive, and rejecting. You see, when you are mad at someone in your past, the people in your present typically get the punishment, whether you intend them to or not. This is especially true of those closest to you.

I want you to do an important exercise. I want you to take out a piece of paper and a pen and write down everyone from your past you haven't forgiven. As you do this, ask the Holy Spirit to help you. Ask Him to remind you of any person you may have forgotten about that you have not forgiven. This could be parents, stepparents, siblings, friends, neighbors, teachers, coaches, bosses, business partners, spouses, ex-spouses, ex-lovers, children, relatives, and more. Be sure to make your list complete.

Now, with your list in hand, forgive all of them. You can do this in three steps. You may have to repeat these steps a number of times for those who really hurt you, but don't stop until you receive a breakthrough and you know it is resolved. You cannot afford unforgiveness in your life.

Repent of unforgiveness

Unforgiveness isn't a little problem; it is a sin. Our sins put Jesus on the cross. On that cross, Jesus forgave those who put Him there and died so our sins could be forgiven. He literally shut the doors of hell and opened the gates of heaven for us through His death. And now, what He requires of us in return is that we forgive others in the same spirit by which we have been forgiven by God. When we won't, it is a sin against God and His grace.

Repent and ask God to forgive you, and He will.

Release the offender from your judgement

When others offend us or those we love, we often put labels on them—jerk, idiot, loser, or something worse. We devalue them and assign a lower degree of worth to them. This allows us to justify our behavior and attitudes toward them.

We also think that we know all about them. We judge their motives, their intelligence, their future intentions, and so on. And because we have judged them, we act accordingly. We reject, revile, and even punish them because it is the inevitable result of judgement. In Matthew 7:1–2, Jesus commands us not to judge and informs us that God will judge us with the same judgement we give to others—justice for justice and mercy for mercy.

Forgiveness means reversing the process I've just described. You must give your offenders a high value and resign as their judge and let God judge them. You must understand that the people you despise or are bitter toward are God's children and that He loves them as much as He loves you. It may sound offensive, but it is true. You must give them a high worth and know that God does also. Renounce the labels and low value you have assigned to them. Also, declare yourself incompetent to judge them. You are! Only God knows their hearts and why they do what they do.

Many years ago, I resented a man I thought was weird. He was causing problems in our church. I had judged him and thought I knew all about him. Then one day, in a conversation with him, I found out that he'd had eleven stepfathers when he was growing up, and many of them had abused him. When I learned that, I was embarrassed because it explained the way he behaved.

I have learned that only God is qualified to judge us and others. Forgiveness is the renunciation of the right of judgement and the recognition of God as the true Judge of all.

We can trust God to judge righteously as we forgive and walk in love.

Bless those you are forgiving until your feelings toward them change

Here is what Jesus says about this issue: "Love your enemies, do good to those who hate you, bless those who curse you, and pray for those who spitefully use you" (Luke 6:27–28).

When it comes to forgiveness, many people think they can't forgive because of the negative feelings that remain after they have followed the first two steps. We must understand that our emotions are the caboose in our walk with the Lord, not the engine. The engine of our faith is our will, and the most important thing to God is that we choose to do what is right regardless of our feelings.

However, our feelings are real, and they are important. In order to be healed from the feelings of bitterness, hate, hurt, and offense, we must follow the commandment of Jesus to bless those who curse us and pray for those who mistreat us.

I haven't truly hated many people in my life, but there have been a few. One of the people I truly hated was a man who tried to keep the elders of our church from choosing me to become the pastor. Not only that, but he also campaigned throughout the church, letting others know how he felt. I hated him and entertained myself privately with thoughts of his demise. At that point, his obituary was my happy thought.

One day, as I prayed, the Lord confronted me about my bitterness and hate. As He did, He spoke to my heart, saying that I needed to bless the man I hated so much. It offended me, and I resisted the Lord in doing it.

Let me also mention that at this point my bitterness was negatively affecting my wife, children, and everyone around me. I was becoming an angry and bitter person, and my personality was changing for the worse.

As the Lord told me to bless that man, I found it to be repugnant. But I finally obeyed. My heart wasn't really in it at first because I didn't want good for that man. I wanted God to kill him for me. But I blessed him and prayed for him in my daily prayer time in obedience to the Lord. Nothing changed for a while, but then one day while I was praying for him, a wave of God's love for him crashed over my heart. In a moment, my bitterness turned to compassion. It was truly miraculous, and from that day forward, I have never again wrestled with negative feelings toward him.

If you will obey God in blessing and praying for those who have offended you or those you love, He will be faithful to heal your emotions so you can go forward with a renewed heart. As you bless others, He will bless you.

Five Steps to Achieving Freedom from Iniquities

The concept of generational sin is introduced early in the Bible. Adam and Eve's sin has affected every generation of people on this planet. It is called "the fall of man." Even though we weren't in the garden and we didn't commit the sin of eating the forbidden fruit with them, we nevertheless suffer because of their sin.

The same truth applies to our parents. Their behavior, both good and bad, has a profound impact on us. Their attitudes, beliefs about God, methods of discipline, and life values constantly impact our developing souls while we are growing up and, to some degree, even after we are grown. When our parents are righteous, it has a positive impact upon us. However, when they are sinful and wrong, the result is an unrighteous influence upon our lives, which normally results in the same sin. Even when we don't follow our parents' sin, our lives are still influenced negatively. The Bible calls this family dynamic "iniquities."

Here is what the Lord says to the children of Israel concerning sin and its consequences in subsequent generations:

> "I, the Lord your God, *am* a jealous God, visiting the
> iniquity of the fathers upon the children to the third and
> fourth *generations* of those who hate Me, but showing
> mercy to thousands, to those who love Me and keep
> My commandments" (Deuteronomy 5:9–10).

Even though this Scripture specifically addresses the iniquities of fathers upon their children, the issue of iniquities relates to mothers as well. In counseling, we find that the transference of iniquities has little to do with gender and much to do with the influence of both parents. The word "fathers" in Deuteronomy 5:9 can also be translated "ancestors," thereby including both sexes.

God's promise to Moses is the visitation of the iniquities of the parents on their children for up to four generations and the blessing of righteousness to thousands. Even though some might raise an eyebrow at the fact that God would allow children to suffer for parental error, we must also look at the incredible blessing children receive when their parents are righteous. Regardless of which side we see, the truth is that the behavior of parents has a profound impact on their children. We see this truth every day in our society as more children reflect the fallen attitudes and sinful cycles of their apostate parents.

But beyond what is clearly evident in others, each of us must deal with iniquities in our own lives in order to be free from our past. I have never met a person, including myself, who didn't have iniquities from his parents to deal with. The word "iniquity" in the Hebrew language is derived from the word *avah*, which means "to bend, twist, or distort." An iniquity is a tendency toward a sin or error because of the influence of one's parents or family history.

Think about what happens to a tree when it is constantly blown in one direction. It grows with a bend in it. The same is true of a child who is raised in a home where sin is present, as we all have been. No one has perfect parents. The degree to which our parents are righteous and normal in their behavior is the same degree to which we are able to grow up "straight" and healthy. However, when they have attitudes or behaviors that are sinful, wrong, or abusive, it creates a direct influence in our lives, which can bend us in a wrong direction.

Because our parents' behavior affects us so directly, we must respond properly to our sins and problems. If we don't, the results will be lifelong manifestations, which will damage our lives and be passed on to our children. If we do, though, we can be free from the sins of our parents and pass that freedom on for generations to come. Therefore, I will show you how to recognize iniquities in your life and in your parents and how to be set free from them as well as how to stop them from influencing your children. Here are the five steps to being set free from iniquities:

Recognize the iniquities

The first step in breaking iniquities is learning to recognize the iniquities of your parents. The principle is simple. An iniquity is any form of behavior you recognize in your parents' lives or family history as being unbiblical, as not being representative of the character of God, and as having a generational influence.

The following is a list of common iniquities people deal with:

- Anger
- Gossip
- Prejudice
- Bitterness
- Judgmentalism
- Unforgiveness
- Chauvinism
- Dominance
- Sexual abuse
- Substance abuse
- Pride
- Fear
- Negativity
- Control
- Manipulation
- Physical Abuse
- Irresponsibility
- Rebellion
- Verbal Abuse
- Moral Impurity
- Codependent Beahvior
- Antiosocial Attitudes and Behavior

This list could fill pages, but the point is this: When you recognize the fact that you have been influenced by a negative trait in your parents, the first thing to do is to call it what it is. Freedom begins with truth.

Forgive

The second step in being set free from iniquities is to forgive our parents. Because I just addressed the issue of forgiveness, I will trust that you understand the steps of how to do this and the importance of it. Forgiveness is the mother of all issues in being set free from our past and our parents' sins.

Repent

Once you have completed the first two steps, the next step is personal repentance. Even though our parents may have wrongly influenced us, we are nevertheless responsible for our own behavior. When we examine ourselves in light of our parents' lives, we must ask ourselves the sobering question: *Am I like them*? If we are, even in a different or lesser fashion, we must repent before God and before others we have harmed through our behavior.

The reason sin destroys families is because we fail to recognize it and deal with it properly. However, if we will call sin what it is, forgive those who have sinned, and repent for our own sins, the blood of Jesus erases the power of that sin from our lives.

A healthy examination for every parent is to consider what things we are doing with our children that could become an iniquity for them later on. If we notice that we are sinning toward our spouse or children or demonstrating unrighteous behavior before them, the answer is to repent before them and God. This has the powerful effect of stopping sin from further influencing our families.

Submit

The next step in gaining freedom from iniquities is to submit ourselves to Jesus. Iniquities begin as parents rebel against God's authority and the truth of His Word. The resulting sin twists and distorts their children's lives and perception of life. The cycle can only be broken by recognizing the original sin and making things right. Once we have identified the sin, forgiven our parents and family, and repented for our behavior to God and others, we must then ask Jesus to heal and change that area of our lives. We need to admit our problem and submit to the Word of God and the work of the Holy Spirit to lead us into truth and straighten us from our bent in that area.

Pray

This step is simple but profound. As you finalize the breaking of iniquities over your life and the lives of generations after you, pray a simple prayer like this:

> Father, I recognize this iniquity and repent of my involvement in it. I forgive my parents for anything they have done wrong, and I bless them. I ask for Your forgiveness and receive it. I also break the power of this iniquity off my life in the name of Jesus. I break [name the iniquity(ies)] off my life and all future generations. I renounce it and pray that You will heal me and teach me how to change this area and walk in obedience to You. I thank You for forgiving me and setting me free. In Jesus' name, Amen.

Three Problems with Inner Vows

An inner vow is a self-oriented commitment made in response to a person, experience, or desire in life. We most often make inner vows in response to pain or frustration. The key issue in understanding and identifying inner vows relates to the "self" nature of the vow. Whenever we focus a commitment inward—that is, toward ourselves, as opposed to upward to God or outward towards others—that commitment becomes an inner vow. Rather than freeing us from a problem or propelling us forward in life, inner vows act as tethers that hinder us and tie us to the past in an unhealthy way.

Here are some common examples of inner vows:

- "No one will ever hurt me again!"
- "I'll never be vulnerable again to anyone."
- "I'm never going to be poor like my parents."
- "I'm never going to allow myself to fall in love with anyone ever again!"
- "I'm never going to trust anyone else in my life."
- "I'll never let anyone else make a fool out of me again!"
- "I'm not going to be strict with my children."
- "I'm going to give my children everything they want."
- "My husband/wife will never treat me like that!"

We make inner vows to comfort ourselves relative to the future. We aren't trying to do something wrong; we are trying to correct something we believe is wrong. However, regardless of how noble our motives are, there are three major problems that arise from inner vows in our lives.

Inner vows are unscriptural.

Here is what Jesus says related to the vows we make:

> "You have heard that it was said to those of old, 'You
> shall not swear falsely, but shall perform your oaths to
> the Lord.' But I say to you, do not swear at all: neither
> by heaven, for it is God's throne; nor by the earth, for it
> is His footstool; nor by Jerusalem, for it is the city of the
> great King. Nor shall you swear by your head, because you
> cannot make one hair white or black. But let your 'Yes' be
> 'Yes,' and your 'No,' 'No.' For whatever is more than these
> is from the evil one" (Matthew 5:33–37).

The main problem with an inner vow is the fact that
it does not have to submit itself to God. Jesus tells us to
"perform your oaths to the Lord." This means that if we are
going to make any significant commitments in our lives,
they are to be focused toward God and fulfilled as an act of
worship and obedience to Him. Inner vows are the exact
opposite.

Made to ourselves, inner vows are self-focused, self-serv-
ing commitments that in many cases resist and oppose
the will of God in our lives. It is possible for Christians
to live their entire lives with four or five major inner
vows operating under the surface of their consciousness
while living with the impression that they are completely
submitted to the Lord.

To be set free from inner vows, we must first understand
that we don't have the right to make vows to ourselves. If
we are sincere in our walk with the Lord, this means that

whatever comes into or goes out of our lives does so under the Lordship of Jesus.

To make an inner vow is to wrest control of one's life away from God and to set one's own course without His approval or blessing. This explains why they are wrong and cause so many problems.

Related to the unscriptural nature of an inner vow is the fact that inner vows are typically tied to a judgement one has made. As I stated earlier in this chapter, judgements have a powerful influence in connecting us to the negative issues of the past. Until we break our judgements and renounce our inner vows and submit them to God, we won't find the peace we are looking for in life.

Inner vows have an unforeseen effect.

When we make an inner vow, we have set a course for our life. Even though we don't spend the bulk of our day thinking about all of the inner vows we've made, they nevertheless have a powerful influence upon us. As unseen forces that guide one's destiny, inner vows have the power to pull the strongest person in a direction he isn't even aware of. Part of the reason is that inner vows also have a "sleeper" effect. After we have made them, they can become a part of our subconscious mind until something happens to trigger them.

One of the most dangerous things about inner vows is that when they are directing our lives, God isn't. In order to give the Lord true authority over our lives, we must first of all make sure there are no inner vows working silently beneath the surface of our thoughts, competing against the Spirit of God.

Inner vows are our highest level of commitment.

When it comes to what people are going to do with their lives, it typically comes down to their priorities and values. Inner vows are the highest level of commitment for most people. Obviously, this isn't the way it should be. Our greatest commitment should be to the Lord. However, when we've sworn to ourselves that we will do something or not do something, that commitment subconsciously overrides any commitment we have to God. This point explains why there are so many precious, sincere Christians who say they love God but have so many areas of their lives operating in such opposition to His purposes. Without even realizing it, they are fulfilling a commitment of their past that has become a competitor with Christ.

We must be careful not to let anything get in the way of our commitment to Jesus Christ. If we realize that there are any commitments we've made to ourselves and withheld from God, we must quickly submit them, lest they keep us from fully giving ourselves to the Lord and serving Him in truth.

In almost all cases in which we have made an inner vow, we go to an opposite extreme in our behavior, thinking we have solved the problem. In truth, because of our inner vow, we become overly vigilant and live in extremes that are often harmful to us and others around us. I compare it to a drunk man trying to get on a horse. In judgment of their parents, one generation after the next keeps falling off, from one side to the other, with inner vows causing them to live from extreme to extreme. One generation is legalistic, so the next is lawless. One generation is frugal, so the next is materialistic. One generation is highly social, so the next is antisocial. And so go the extremes until a person arises who breaks his or her inner vows and finally mounts the horse to live in balance and truth.

How to Achieve Freedom from Inner Vows

The first key to unlocking inner vows from your life is to think back on any failures of your parents or other important people in your life or any other negative circumstances from your past. As you are remembering, think about your response. Did you make promises to yourself about God, relationships, money, pain, or anything else? Did you make strong judgements about your past, your parents, or your future?

When you recognize specific judgements and resulting vows you made to yourself while growing up or even as an adult, renounce the inner vow and repent for letting it take charge of your life. Then take the area of your life in question and submit it to God. If there is a change to be made, ask God to reveal that to you. If you know that what you have experienced is wrong, ask God to teach you how to do it properly. However, the main point is that your responses or commitments in life are not to be directed to you but to God.

Also, in unlocking our inner vows, we must release our judgements and unforgiveness for the people in our past. Almost all inner vows go back to some level of judgmentalism and unforgiveness. If we have made inner vows, we almost always have someone to forgive and judgements to break.

In every victory and in all suffering, God waits to help us and bless us. Whenever we reject the wise counsel and grace of God in the events of our lives, we are making a terrible mistake. Inner vows, no matter how innocent or seemingly meaningless, are direct threats to the Lordship of Christ and His will for our lives. They threaten to distract us from God and pull our loyalties away from Him and toward our own self-governing agendas.

Have you made any inner vows that are silently steering your life today? If you have, identify them and break them. Even if your inner vow has a positive and healthy commitment attached to it, it should be made to the Lord, not to yourself. As you honestly examine your own heart and break the inner vows from your past, you take one more step toward becoming free to fulfill God's will for your life.

Freedom from your past is a big deal. Unforgiveness, iniquities, and inner vows act as invisible chains that bind us to negative past events.

Now that you are free and have taken this important step, you are ready for the final step toward Christ.

10

Winning the Battle for Your Mind

You will keep *him* in perfect peace,
Whose mind *is* stayed on *You*,
Because he trusts in You.

—Isaiah 26:3

When they crucified Jesus, they nailed Him to a cross and placed it on a hill called Golgotha. Golgotha means "the place of a skull." I've been to Jerusalem and seen Golgotha. It is eerie. As you view this hill from a distance, it looks just like a human skull. On the day Jesus was crucified, He hung on a cross positioned prominently on the top of a hill shaped like a skull. This was no accident. It was orchestrated by God to reveal a central truth of the reason Christ died.

The primary battlefield in our daily lives is in our minds. This is why God chose the setting for the crucifixion as a place that had the name and appearance of a human skull. He could have chosen a hill that looked like an eye, heart, arm, or foot, but He didn't. Jesus died on the top of a skull-shaped hill to demonstrate the purpose of His death. Once His mission was accomplished and He breathed His last, they pierced Him in the side; blood and water spilled out and landed on the ground they called "a skull."

We cannot overlook this powerful picture. You see, Jesus died to save us and set us free. Our minds are a central issue in the battle for our salvation and resulting freedom. The truth of the matter is that until our minds are set free, we're not free. Until the transforming power of the blood of Jesus and the water of His word flow upon our minds, we are in bondage.

Francis Frangipane once said, "A bondage is a house of thoughts." This is a truth that we must understand if we are going to win the battle for our minds. An example is sexual bondage. Many people think the issue is primarily biological or hormonal. Therefore, they try to fight their sexual impulses through physical discipline or willpower. Even the strongest person with the greatest amount of willpower can last for only a certain period of time until he or she is worn down and defeated. Thousands of years of human history prove that sexual sin can take the best people down. The story of David and Bathsheba demonstrates this point (2 Samuel 11).

To solve a problem, you have to deal with the root issue before you can find a real solution. In other words, if you have a problem but are unaware of the true source of it, either you will try false answers that don't work, or you will believe that no answer exists. This is the predicament for most people relative to chronic problems such as fear, worry, sexual bondage, eating disorders, depression, and so on. They either try false answers that only have a temporary effect on their behavior, or they give themselves over to their problems or sinful desires, believing that no solution exists because everything they tried has failed.

In any area of our lives, we will not be set free until we deal with the root issue of our problems. And in almost every instance, the real problem is the way we think.

The Promise of Freedom

Here is what Jesus says concerning freedom: "If you abide in My word, you are My disciples indeed. And you shall know the truth, and the truth shall make you free" (John 8:31–32). Jesus clearly states that true freedom is the result of abiding in His Word. He promises that if we become committed disciples of His Word, we will know the truth, and the result will be freedom. The word "know" in the Greek language doesn't just mean "to understand." It means "to experience intimately." Therefore, Jesus promises that if we will commit our minds and hearts to His Word, the result will be a personal experience that sets us free.

Freedom is available for anyone in any bondage or battle of life. However, it must first take place in our minds. Many people try and fail when it comes to changing a behavior or stopping a sin in their lives because they rely on their will instead of their minds. Sure, the will has to be involved, but it can't work independently from our minds or override the powerful force of our thoughts.

The stage was set all the way back in Genesis 3, when Satan first attacked mankind in the Garden of Eden. He didn't defeat them with bombs, guns, or physical force. Satan's weapon of choice then and now is mental deception. As a cunning serpent, he seeks to silently introduce into our minds seductive thoughts that we will accept. A perfect example is pornography. With pornography, Satan presents his destructive deception in a package that is enticing. However, even though you might not realize it, pornography isn't about nakedness, beautiful men and women, or sex. It is a multilayered system of Satanic deception that refutes God's Word and His will concerning the sacred nature of sex, the character of God, the role of men and women, the marriage covenant, love, and human fulfillment. Until we realize what pornography is really about and attack the thought system behind it, we will never be free.

The Sword of the Spirit

We also need to realize that the battle isn't between the devil and us. Even though our minds are the battlefield, the real fight is between God's Word and Satan. As long as we think the issue is about us, we will try to fight it ourselves. We must understand that we are helpless against Satan without God's Word. Ephesians 6:17 tells us that the Word is the "sword of the Spirit" in our fight against the forces of darkness. It is nuclear in the realm of the spirit and can defeat any enemy. We must not try to win with our own strength or abilities. We must believe in the power of God's Word and let it do its work in us and for us.

Someone might be thinking, "Well, I know a lot of people who aren't religious and don't believe in the Bible, and they aren't in bondage to sex or things like that." Sure, not everyone in the world has the same bondages. However, you show me a person who doesn't live with a close, personal dependence upon God's Word, and I'll show you someone who is defeated and in bondage. The bondage might not be sex, but it's fear, depression, hate, or something else.

No one is the exception when it comes to the importance of depending on God's Word—not even Jesus. Matthew 4 records the temptation of Christ after 40 days of fasting in the wilderness. In this weak moment, Satan comes to attempt to defeat the Son of God. What does he attack Him with? Thoughts! Three times Satan attacks Jesus with half-truths and seductive offers. Every time, Jesus counters with a response beginning with "It is written." Demonstrating the awesome power of God's Word over Satan's best attack, Jesus wins and teaches us how to do the same.

To help us understand the battle of our minds and how it is won, the apostle Paul gives us rare spiritual insight. He says,

> Though we walk in the flesh, we do not war according to the flesh. For the weapons of our warfare *are* not carnal but mighty in God for pulling down strongholds, casting down arguments and every high thing that exalts itself against the knowledge of God, bringing every thought into captivity to the obedience of Christ (2 Corinthians 10:3–5).

These verses accurately describe the reality of the battlefield of our minds and the way to win the war for our freedom. Even though it's true, the greatest obstacle to victory is the fact that the weapons and the war Paul describes can't be seen and must be entered into by faith. Let's face it—it's hard for us to believe in the power of weapons that are invisible.

It's also difficult for us to fight an enemy we can't see. However, that is exactly what we must do if we are going to live in victory.

Paul tells us that we have weapons of warfare available to us that are "not carnal." Our weapons are not physical or natural; they are spiritual and invisible. He goes on to say that these weapons are "mighty in God for pulling down strongholds."

God has given us powerful spiritual weapons to overcome every stronghold Satan has brought into our lives to keep us in bondage. However, the power of these weapons will work only in an atmosphere of faith in which we are willing to obediently enter the battle of our minds.

Look again at Paul's language in 2 Corinthians 10. He tells us that we must bring "every thought captive to the obedience of Christ." This literally means that every thought in our minds must submit to the authority of Jesus Christ—the Word (John 1:1). Any thought that we won't take captive will take us captive by building strongholds of "arguments" and "high things that exalt themselves against the knowledge of God." By faith, we must fight against any and every thought that won't bow its knee to Christ. These thoughts are our real enemies.

The battle for freedom is waged in "the place of a skull." Until your mind is completely surrendered to Christ and you are willing to seek and accept His Word as truth, you aren't ready for freedom and can't obtain it by any other means. However, if you're willing to bring your mind to Christ and cast down the arguments (thoughts that reject the truth of God's Word), surrender the high things (prideful thinking that believes it has a better answer than God's Word), and bring every thought captive, you are ready for freedom.

The Power of Biblical Meditation

The book of Psalms begins with this powerful description of the person who has committed his or her mind to biblical meditation:

> Blessed *is* the man
> Who walks not in the counsel of the ungodly,
>> Nor stands in the path of sinners,
>> Nor sits in the seat of the scornful;
> But his delight *is* in the law of the Lord,
> And in His law he meditates day and night.
> He shall be like a tree
>> Planted by the rivers of water,
>> That brings forth its fruit in its season,
>> Whose leaf also shall not wither;
> And whatever he does shall prosper (Psalm 1:1–3).

Biblical meditation simply means rehearsing God's Word in our minds. The picture is of a sheep that regurgitates its food and keeps rechewing it until it is finally digested. As we recall Scriptures at key times of the day and night and think upon them, we are meditating and qualify for the blessings promised in Psalm 1.

The power of biblical meditation is so great that God promises everything we do will prosper if we will practice it "day and night." This is a promise too great to ignore. Can you imagine everything in your life prospering and succeeding?

Psalm 1:3 compares a person who meditates on Scripture day and night to a tree planted by a river. The tree doesn't have to worry about whether the rains come because it has a stable source of water to keep it healthy and fruitful. The result is guaranteed success—just as God promises all of us if we will meditate on Scripture.

Many people beat their way through life trying to make it. Unlike a tree by a river, they look and feel more like a bush in the desert. Failure and frustration become so common that the thought of guaranteed success seems like an unrealistic dream. However, it's not a dream; it's a promise. This promise comes with one condition: that you refuse ungodly counsel and meditate upon God's Word day and night. If biblical meditation were the most difficult thing you ever did in your life, wouldn't it be worthwhile if it guaranteed success in everything you did—work, money, relationships, sex, and so on?

I want to give you some really good news. Not only does biblical meditation guarantee success, but it is also easy and you can do it. When I first heard about it, I thought to myself, *I don't think I can do that.* I also thought, *I don't know if I want to do that*! I just couldn't imagine sitting around thinking about the Bible all of the time. Sure, I loved God and believed in the Bible, but to think about it all day and night—wow! I didn't think I was up to it. That was many years ago. Now I can't believe how hard it was not doing it. I regret every day of my unbelief and procrastination. It caused me so much needless defeat and suffering.

Misunderstanding biblical meditation scares most people away. They think it is either impractical or too spiritually difficult for them. The truth is any man, woman, or child can meditate upon Scripture day and night. In this chapter, I will erase the myths and misunderstandings concerning this powerful practice. I will also give you practical information to demonstrate how you can do it in the midst of your demanding lifestyle.

I want you to know that regardless of what you've experienced in your past, your future can be full of great blessing and success. If you can just meet the condition set forth in Psalm 1, God promises His blessing of success in everything you do. You owe it to yourself to consider this issue carefully because of the powerful blessings being offered through the discipline of biblical meditation.

One great blessing is the power to live in sexual purity.

Sexual Purity

Let me share with you a powerful truth concerning your mind and sexual temptation. Did you know that you cannot take a thought out of your mind? That's right—it's impossible. This is why sexual temptation is so wearying to try to fight.

An example is this: You are minding your own business as you're flipping through the television channels, and then all of a sudden there he or she is—a perfect 10! From head to toe, this person is gorgeous and sexy, and this person is looking at you with that *wanting* stare. You pause for a few minutes and take it all in. Later, you turn off the television and go to bed, but the image is still in your mind.

You lie in bed thinking about the person you saw. Then you realize that what you're doing is wrong, and you begin feeling guilty. However, you just can't get the thought of the person out of your mind. The more you try, the worse it gets. In fact, the more you try, the more other sinful thoughts and images begin to surface, and the battle is raging. Finally, you give in and let your mind go where you know it shouldn't. Defeated and guilty, you go to sleep, only to wake up to another day to fight the same futile battle. You want to live for God and be faithful to your spouse, but can you ever be strong enough to overcome these thoughts that have conquered you for so long?

If you can relate to this, I have some good news for you. You can have the power to overcome these undesirable thoughts and to exercise complete control over your mind. To do so, you must remember this: you cannot take thoughts out of your mind, but you can crowd them out with more powerful thoughts. This is where biblical meditation comes in.

Most people wrestle constantly with their thought lives. Many times we know that the things we think about are wrong, but we don't know how to stop them. It can be worry, fear, anger, sexual temptation, or many other issues. We don't ask for them; they're just there, waiting for us. To make matters worse, the more we try to stop thinking about them, the more they occupy our thinking. Satan loves this vicious cycle because he wants to turn our minds inward until they wear out, we give up, and he controls us.

Efforts to change become futile, so we just give in and become like everyone else. This is also why so many people turn to alcohol or drugs and escape through some form of pleasure or distraction. It is the only way they know to cope with their internal miseries.

Before I came into the ministry, I worked in my family's business. On my way to work every day, I passed a billboard for a swimming pool company. It was a very large sign with a woman in a swimsuit filling most of it. Whoever painted her wasn't just a good artist but was also intimately familiar with the female body and went to great pains to include every detail. As I passed the sign each day, I looked. In fact, I became so distracted by the sign that I would slow down before I got to it, hoping to hit a red light so I could look longer.

Eventually, the image on that billboard became fixed in my mind whether I was sitting in front of it or not. One morning, as I was trying to pray and have a quiet time with the Lord, the image of that sign flashed in my mind. (Satan loves to do this to Christians when they are trying to worship in church, read the Bible, or pray because he doesn't want us to get close to God.) When this image came into my mind, I confessed it to the Lord and told Him I didn't want to think about it anymore but didn't know how to stop it.

The Lord spoke to my heart right then and said something that began my journey to freedom from sexual temptation: "Whenever this thought or any other temptation comes into your mind, begin to meditate on My Word." From that moment on, I began overcoming sexual temptation. I'm not saying I never sinned again; I'm saying that I started a pattern of winning more battles than I lost by knowing how to win every time by meditating on Scripture.

You can't get bad thoughts out of your mind with your own thoughts or some method of mind control or distraction. If you do, your success will be short lived, and the thoughts will come back with a greater fury than before. The only power that can truly set you free is biblical meditation. This is why

God promises success in every area of life for the person who does it day and night.

Make up your mind right now that the next time a bad thought comes into your mind, you are going to replace it with a Scripture. Even more important, you will realize that the more you meditate on Scripture before you are tempted, the less opportunity Satan has to tempt you in the first place. You see, biblical meditation fills your mind with God's Word. Therefore, it is no longer unoccupied and open for the enemy's attacks. As the old saying goes, "An idle mind is the devil's playground." In reality, an idle mind is the devil's battleground where he assaults and defeats his victims.

Timing Is Everything

Another important issue is understanding how to practically meditate on the Word of God "day and night," as Psalm 1:2 describes. If you misunderstand this point, you will get discouraged and give up before you start. However, once you understand what God's Word is saying, you will realize its brilliance and practicality.

To understand this issue, let's look at something God says through Moses to the children of Israel as they prepare to enter the Promised Land.

> "Hear, O Israel: The Lord our God, the Lord *is* one! You
> shall love the Lord your God with all your heart, with all
> your soul, and with all your strength.
>   And these words which I command you today shall
> be in your heart. You shall teach them diligently to your
> children, and shall talk of them when you sit in your

house, when you walk by the way, when you lie down, and when you rise up" (Deuteronomy 6:4–7).

What can we learn from this? God's first commandment to Israel is for them to love Him and His Word with their whole heart, soul, and strength. Likewise, we must totally commit ourselves to God before we can live victoriously. The second thing God commands the men of Israel to do is to diligently teach their children the Word of God. God still holds us responsible to train our children in the Word and ways of God (Ephesians 6:4).

The interesting thing about God's commandment to train children in the Word is that God details for them the four times of the day and night in which they are to do it. In Deuteronomy 6:7, God directs Israel to teach their children His Word and to talk about it when they (1) are sitting in their houses, (2) are on their way somewhere, (3) rise up in the morning, and (4) go to bed at night. How practical!

Think about the times when you are tempted and struggle with your thoughts the most. I'll tell you when it is. It is when your mind is in an unoccupied and reflective mode. You probably don't have as much problem with your thoughts when you are busy at work or directly occupied by a task. It's not to say you can't have problems during those times; it's just not as common because you are mentally occupied.

The times our minds are most open to satanic assault are when we are sitting around our houses (channel surfing, Web surfing, or whatever), on our way somewhere (in the car looking at billboards, noticing the person in the car next to us, daydreaming), and lying in bed as we wake up and go to sleep (worrying about our problems, fantasizing about our sinful desires). Let me guess. You just got nailed, right? We all did. God knew thousands of years ago, before there were televisions, computers, cars, or billboards, that we were most vulnerable at four times of the day. He also knew those same four times were the best opportunity for us to meditate on Scripture as we learn it for ourselves and teach it to our children.

Needless to say, most people today don't live as God directed in Deuteronomy. That is why Satan has so much success in his attacks on our minds. For hours each day, most of us sit in our homes and cars and lie in our beds with our minds vacant and vulnerable.

Meditating on God's Word "day and night" means we are committed to occupying our minds with the Word of God during the four reflective times of our day mentioned in Deuteronomy 6:7. This doesn't mean we are legalistic and can't watch television, rent a movie, surf the Web, or listen to music. It just means that God's Word comes before any of those things and that when we encounter a sinful thought through television, computers, movies, or anything else, we take it captive and replace it with a Scripture we have readily waiting in our minds

If you are dealing with fear, for example, you need to find Scriptures about overcoming fear and have them ready in your mind when the attacks and temptations come. 2 Timothy 1:7 tells us, "God has not given us a spirit of fear, but of power and of love and of a sound mind." With that Scripture loaded into your mind at the beginning of the day, you are now empowered to win the battle for your mind.

You can apply this to any other area of your life. At the back of this book, there is an appendix with Scriptures for confession and meditation. I have included Scriptures for many of the issues you may be dealing with right now. Again, biblical meditation is practical. You read what you need! Are you dealing with discouragement? Then find encouraging Scriptures and keep them ready for battle when the enemy comes against you. Are you dealing with physical problems? Then find Scriptures about God's healing power and meditate upon them and confess them throughout the day.

Once you grasp this truth and begin putting it into practice, you will realize how powerful it is. Life is more pleasant and peaceful when you learn to meditate upon Scripture. You realize that you can defeat the enemy anytime he comes against you and that you can live your life free from mental turmoil and temptation. You also realize the power of the Word of God. As you meditate on it, the Word unfolds within you, and you begin to see its beauty and understand its mysteries. The Bible is no longer a difficult book you have a hard time getting into. It becomes your life source, and you begin longing for it.

Most of what I know about the Bible I have learned while driving in my car, sitting in my house, or lying in my bed meditating on a Scripture. Not only has my mind been protected by biblical meditation, but also it has been enlightened and prepared for success. Truly, biblical meditation has changed my life, and God has fulfilled His promise to prosper me in all of my ways. He will also do the same for you.

You are now empowered to win the battle for your mind. You have also taken your tenth step! I pray that you feel closer to Christ than ever before. He loves you and has a great plan and purpose for your life. Trust Him and keep walking with Him every day.

You are destined for success and victory.

Appendix I

Leading a Small Group

Start the Journey

Thank you for being part of the journey. Every year many people make a trip to the altar for salvation, only to end up leaving the faith frustrated. Why? Because they can't seem to enjoy the new freedoms promised in a life for Christ. *Ten Steps Toward Christ* is meant to help people take some basic steps to ensure success. However, any person who has committed to "run the race" knows that no amount of knowledge will help without a group of people encouraging them when they struggle. So thank you for being willing to start the trip and encourage your brothers and sisters in Christ.

For those of you who've never led a group like this, we've put together a few pointers.

Have a Clear Direction

There is no expectation that each person in the group will come out a perfect Christian at the end. The point is to get people walking toward Christ in their daily lives. The group is on a journey. Have fun. Get to know each other and keep walking toward Christ.

The book is divided into 10 steps that take the group from "being born again" all the way to being capable of "winning the battle" for their hearts and minds. Take a look at the chapter headings to get a clear sense of the direction you'll be leading the group. Be aware that not every question can be answered in one conversation but will likely be answered at some point down the road.

Emphasize Prayer and Meditation

It's been said that the Bible is a road map, and spending time with the Holy Spirit in prayer and meditation is a compass. In prayer, the Holy Spirit will let you know if you're taking the group in the right direction or may even prompt you to take a rest stop and share something specifically for the group or one of its members. Ultimately, even though you may be the person in charge of the group, the Holy Spirit is really the one leading, which takes a lot of pressure off of you. Take advantage of what God offers you through prayer.

Read the Chapters

Christianity isn't a trip to be breezed through at 70 miles per hour. It's meant to be savored. You're the tour guide for the group, so know the tour stops and help the group enjoy each place. Read the Scriptures in each chapter and be ready to help the group understand why each stop is important.

Have Fun

Finally, enjoy yourself. This is a chance to get to know your family in Christ. Make memories, tell jokes, and just have fun!

Step 1: Being Born Again

Big Idea

Have you been born again?

Introduction

Jimmy discussed his own personal journey toward finding Christ. We all have a unique story of being born again, and some of us are still watching the story unfold. The apostle Peter challenges us in 1 Peter to be ready to share our story and testify of the hope it brings to our lives.

Scripture

1 Peter 3:15
But sanctify the Lord God in your hearts, and always be ready to give a defense to everyone who asks you a reason for the hope that is in you, with meekness and fear.

2 Corinthians 5:17
Therefore, if anyone *is* in Christ, *he is* a new creation; old things have passed away; behold, all things have become new.

Discussion

- What does it mean to be "born again"?
- In three minutes or less, share your story of being born again.
- How did this experience influence your daily life?
- What lifestyle changes did you have to make?

Activation

- What can you do this week to live life born again?
- Are there relationships you need to change in order to leave the "old life" behind you?
- Who can you be praying for in your family to be born again?

Step 2: Water Baptism and Communion

Big Idea

What is the importance of baptism and communion?

Introduction

Getting baptized and participating in communion are important first steps after being saved. They demonstrate our sincerity and desire to be a part of the community of Christians and will always remind us that we have been born again as new creations in Christ.

Scripture

Matthew 28:19–20
"Go therefore and make disciples of all the nations, baptizing them in the name of the Father and of the Son and of the Holy Spirit, teaching them to observe all things that I have commanded you; and lo, I am with you always, *even* to the end of the age." Amen.

Luke 22:19–20

And He took bread, gave thanks and broke *it*, and gave *it* to them, saying, "This is My body which is given for you; do this in remembrance of Me." Likewise He also *took* the cup after supper, saying, "This cup *is* the new covenant in My blood, which is shed for you."

Discussion

- Why do you think God commanded us to be baptized?
- What does baptism represent to you?
- What is the importance of communion to you?
- Understanding this topic, how does it affect your daily life?

Activation

- Have you been water baptized? If not, what is holding you back?
- Do you take communion regularly?

Step 3: Baptism in the Holy Spirit

Big Idea

Why do you need to be baptized in the Holy Spirit?

Introduction

God promised that His followers would experience power and supernatural blessings when they were baptized in the Holy Spirit. The benefits of the Holy Spirit are many, including love, joy, peace, patience, kindness, goodness, gentleness, faithfulness, and self-control. But this experience is separate from being born again. Have you been baptized in the Holy Spirit?

Scripture

Matthew 3:11

"I indeed baptize you with water unto repentance, but He who is coming after me is mightier than I, whose sandals I am not worthy to carry. He will baptize you with the Holy Spirit and fire."

Mark 1:8

"I indeed baptized you with water, but He will baptize you with the Holy Spirit."

Discussion

- Why do you need the help of the Holy Spirit in your everyday life?
- How does being baptized in the Holy Spirit affect your daily life?

Activation

- Have you been baptized in the Holy Spirit? If not, what is holding you back?
- What can you do this week to allow the Holy Spirit to work in your life?
- What is hindering you from walking fully in the Holy Spirit?

Step 4: Christian Fellowship

Big Idea

How necessary is good Christian fellowship?

Introduction

Christian friendships are key to growing in faith. They inspire us, encourage us, and sometimes even frustrate us. God designed our faith to be learned and lived through relationships with others who are on the same journey. Do you have good friendships with Christians?

Scripture

Hebrews 10:25
Not forsaking the assembling of ourselves together, as is the manner of some, but exhorting one another, and so much the more as you see the Day approaching.

Matthew 18:20
"For where two or three are gathered together in My name, I am there in the midst of them."

Discussion

- What did fellowship look like for Jesus and the disciples?
- Who are some friends who have influenced your life in times of need?
- What is life like without Christian fellowship?

Activation

- Do you have good friends in your life?
- What can you do this week to be a good friend?
- What relationships are hindering your Christian fellowship?

Step 5: Knowing God through His Word

Big Idea

Can you live as a Christian without God's Word?

Introduction

As a disciple of Jesus, we must know His Word, and to do this we must discipline ourselves to read it daily on our own. It can heal us, adjust our hearts to love God more, empower us, and give us hope in the eternal promises of God. Whatever time and energy we invest in knowing God's Word will pay off eternally.

Scripture

2 Timothy 3:16–17

All Scripture is given by inspiration of God, and is profitable for doctrine, for reproof, for correction, for instruction in righteousness, that the man of God may be complete, thoroughly equipped for every good work.

Hebrews 4:12

For the word of God is living and powerful, and sharper than any two-edged sword, piercing even to the division of soul and spirit, and of joints and marrow, and is a discerner of the thoughts and intents of the heart.

Discussion

- How does reading your Bible help you connect with God?
- Do you have examples of how the Bible has helped you make important decisions?
- How does God speak through His Word?
- What does your Bible reading time look like?

Activation

- Do you have time set aside to read your Bible daily?
- What tools can you use to make your Bible reading more effective?

Step 6: A Dynamic, Daily Prayer Life

Big Idea

Why did Jesus give us an outline for prayer rather than just a prayer to memorize and repeat?

Introduction

Being a Christian is about having a personal relationship with God. And prayer is meant to be a foundation in that relationship, just like conversations are foundational to friendships and marriages. Prayer bonds our hearts to God, nourishes our souls, and produces results in our daily lives.

Scripture

John 14:13–14

"And whatever you ask in My name, that I will do, that the Father may be glorified in the Son. If you ask anything in My name, I will do *it*."

Philippians 4:6

Be anxious for nothing, but in everything by prayer and supplication, with thanksgiving, let your requests be made known to God.

Colossians 4:2

Continue earnestly in prayer, being vigilant in it with thanksgiving.

Discussion

- What are the six parts of the Lord's prayer? (Matt. 6:9–13)
- Why does prayer begin with praise and worship?
- By what name does Jesus teach us to address God? Why is this important?

Activation

- It's important to spend time alone in prayer. When do you have time in your day that you could devote to praying?

Step 7: Stewardship

Big Idea

What does it mean to be a steward?

Introduction

Jesus Christ was a perfect steward of God's will. In fact, Jesus said, "I do nothing of Myself; but as My Father taught me, I speak these things" (John 8:28). One of the great honors of being a Christian is the opportunity to know and do what God desires in our relationships, finances, and communities.

Scripture

Matthew 6:20–21
"But lay up for yourselves treasures in heaven, where neither moth nor rust destroys and where thieves do not break in and steal. For where your treasure is, there your heart will be also."

Luke 12:34

"For where your treasure is, there your heart will be also."

Discussion

- Why do you think the Bible says that our hearts follow our treasures?
- If God ultimately owns everything, then what is our responsibility with the stuff we have?
- What other things besides money should we steward for God?
- Why should we surrender our entire lives?

Activation

- List three things you consider to be the most important in your daily life.
- How can you use these things for the kingdom of God?

Step 8: Hearing God

Big Idea

How does a person hear God?

Introduction

No relationship works without communication that goes both ways. We've already learned about prayer in which we talk to God, but God also can and does speak to us. Some things can drown out what God is saying to us; however, if we practice and listen, then we will be able to hear His still, small voice.

Scripture

Romans 10:17
So then faith *comes* by hearing, and hearing by the word of God.

Colossians 3:15
And let the peace of God rule in your hearts, to which also you were called in one body; and be thankful.

Discussion

- What are some things that keep us from hearing God?
- According to the Bible, how does God speak to us?
- How important is reading the Bible when it comes to hearing God?
- How can we tell the difference between our voice and God's voice?

Activation

- What are some daily activities you can practice to learn the voice of God?
- List some people you would trust in relationship to help you hear the voice of God. Why did you choose these people?

Step 9: Freedom from Your Past

Big Idea

Why do we need freedom from our past?

Introduction

When we are "born again," we become a new person, or what the Bible calls "a new creation." However, beginning a new life can be difficult when we have habits and baggage from our old life. Fortunately, there are ways we can leave behind the old man and enjoy the freedoms of our new life in Christ.

Scripture

Matthew 6:14–15

"For if you forgive men their trespasses, your heavenly Father will also forgive you. But if you do not forgive men their trespasses, neither will your Father forgive your trespasses."

Discussion

- Why is forgiveness such a big deal in starting a new life?
- What does Jesus say about forgiving our enemies?

- What is an iniquity, and where does it come from?
- What causes us to make inner vows, and how does Christ enable us to get over them?

Activation

- Write down a list of everyone you haven't forgiven. Pray that the Holy Spirit would remind you of any person you may have forgotten.
- Write down a list of behaviors in your family history that don't represent the loving and wise character of God. Do you exhibit any of these behaviors in your relationships, jobs, or regular activities?
- Inner vows are promises you make to yourself about God, relationships, money, etc. that don't line up with the Bible. Pray and ask the Holy Spirit to help you see your own inner vows.

Step 10: Winning the Battle for Your Mind

Big Idea

Why is the mind the central battleground that Christ must help us win?

Introduction

Don't be mistaken; we have an enemy in the devil. He's lurking to kill, steal, and destroy our new lives in Christ, and he starts by waging war on our minds. Thankfully, God gives us the weapons and strategies to win this battle so that we can be transformed and victorious.

Scripture

2 Corinthians 10:3–5

For though we walk in the flesh, we do not war according to the flesh. For the weapons of our warfare are not carnal but mighty in God for pulling down strongholds, casting down arguments and every high thing that exalts itself against the knowledge of God, bringing every thought into captivity to the obedience of Christ.

Discussion

- What tools do we have to "take every thought into captivity to the obedience of Christ"?
- What kinds of success in the battles of our minds can we expect if we meditate daily on the Bible? Share any personal example you might have.
- What is the benefit of this daily diligence?

Activation

- Write down a short passage of Scripture that has become meaningful to you over the past few weeks. Carry it with you to work, to lunch, and back home. Set times that you can stop and think about what it says.

Appendix II

Scriptures for Meditation

Here is a list of some suggested Scriptures you can meditate on in dealing with specific issues you may face. This is certainly not an exhaustive list. There are hundreds more verses besides these that will equip you for victory in every area of life. This list of Scriptures will provide a starting point in some of the common areas most of us face. I hope they are helpful to you.

Lust/Immorality
Psalm 101
Proverbs 5:15–21
Proverbs 6:20–7:27
1 Corinthians 6:13–20

Worry/Anxiety
Isaiah 40:31
Matthew 6:24–34
Matthew 11:28–30
Philippians 4:6–7

Fear

Psalm 91

Isaiah 26:3

2 Timothy 1:7

Anger/Unforgiveness

Proverbs 14:17

Proverbs 15:1

Matthew 18:21–35

1 Corinthians 13

Galatians 5:22–23

Ephesians 4:26–27

Discouragement

Joshua 1:89

Romans 5:35

Galatians 6:9

Hebrews 12

Condemnation

Psalm 103:8–14

Romans 8:14

2 Corinthians 12:9

Ephesians 2:48

1 John 1:9

Revelation 12:10–11

Insecurity

Psalm 46:13

Philippians 4:13

Marriage Problems

Ephesians 5:21–33

1 Peter 3:1–12

Pride

Matthew 23:11–12

Mark 9:35

James 4:6–10

Financial Issues

Psalm 37

Proverbs 10:22

Malachi 3:8–12

Matthew 6:19–24

Luke 12:13–21

1 Timothy 6:6–12

Appendix III

Daily Reading Guide

Day 1	Luke 5:27–39	Gen. 1–2	Ps. 1
Day 2	Luke 6:1–26	Gen. 3–5	Ps. 2
Day 3	Luke 6:27–49	Gen. 6–7	Ps. 3
Day 4	Luke 7:1–17	Gen. 8–10	Ps. 4
Day 5	Luke 7:18–50	Gen. 11	Ps. 5
Day 6	Luke 8:1–25	Gen. 12	Ps. 6
Day 7	Luke 8:26–56	Gen. 13–14	Ps. 7
Day 8	Luke 9:1–27	Gen. 15	Ps. 8
Day 9	Luke 9:28–62	Gen. 16	Ps. 9
Day 10	Luke 10:1–20	Gen. 17	Ps. 10
Day 11	Luke 10:21–42	Gen. 18	Ps. 11
Day 12	Luke 11:1–28	Gen. 19	Ps. 12
Day 13	Luke 11:29–54	Gen. 20	Ps. 13
Day 14	Luke 12:1–31	Gen. 21	Ps. 14
Day 15	Luke 12:32–59	Gen. 22	Ps. 15
Day 16	Luke 13:1–17	Gen. 23	Ps. 16
Day 17	Luke 13:18–35	Gen. 24	Ps. 17
Day 18	Luke 14:1–24	Gen. 25	Ps. 18
Day 19	Luke 14:25–35	Gen. 26	Ps. 19
Day 20	Luke 15	Gen. 27:1–45	Ps. 20
Day 21	Luke 16	Gen. 27:46–28:22	Ps. 21
Day 22	Luke 17	Gen. 29:1–30	Ps. 22

Day 23	Luke 18:1–17	Gen. 29:31–30:43	Ps. 23
Day 24	Luke 18:18–43	Gen. 31	Ps. 24
Day 25	Luke 19:1–27	Gen. 32–33	Ps. 25
Day 26	Luke 19:28–48	Gen. 34	Ps. 26
Day 27	Luke 20:1–26	Gen. 35–36	Ps. 27
Day 28	Luke 20:27–47	Gen. 37	Ps. 28
Day 29	Luke 21	Gen. 38	Ps. 29
Day 30	Luke 22:1–38	Gen. 39	Ps. 30
Day 31	Luke 22:39–71	Gen. 40	Ps. 31
Day 32	Luke 23:1–25	Gen. 41	Ps. 32
Day 33	Luke 23:26–56	Gen. 42	Ps. 33
Day 34	Luke 24:1–12	Gen. 43	Ps. 34
Day 35	Luke 24:13–53	Gen. 44	Ps. 35
Day 36	Heb. 1	Gen. 45:1–46:27	Ps. 36
Day 37	Heb. 2	Gen. 46:28–47:31	Ps. 37
Day 38	Heb. 3:1–4:13	Gen. 48	Ps. 38
Day 39	Heb. 4:14–6:12	Gen. 49–50	Ps. 39
Day 40	Heb. 6:13–20	Exod. 1–2	Ps. 40
Day 41	Heb. 7	Exod. 3–4	Ps. 41
Day 42	Heb. 8	Exod. 5:1–6:27	Prov. 1
Day 43	Heb. 9:1–22	Exod. 6:28–8:32	Prov. 2
Day 44	Heb. 9:23–10:18	Exod. 9–10	Prov. 3
Day 45	Heb. 10:19–39	Exod. 11–12	Prov. 4
Day 46	Heb. 11:1–22	Exod. 13–14	Prov. 5
Day 47	Heb. 11:23–40	Exod. 15	Prov. 6:1–7:5
Day 48	Heb. 12	Exod. 16–17	Prov. 7:6–27
Day 49	Heb. 13	Exod. 18–19	Prov. 8
Day 50	Matt. 1	Exod. 20–21	Prov. 9
Day 51	Matt. 2	Exod. 22–23	Prov. 10
Day 52	Matt. 3	Exod. 24	Prov. 11
Day 53	Matt. 4	Exod. 25–27	Prov. 12
Day 54	Matt. 5:1–20	Exod. 28–29	Prov. 13

Day 55	Matt. 5:21–48	Exod. 30–32	Prov. 14
Day 56	Matt. 6:1–18	Exod. 33–34	Prov. 15
Day 57	Matt. 6:19–34	Exod. 35–36	Prov. 16
Day 58	Matt. 7	Exod. 37–38	Prov. 17
Day 59	Matt. 8:1–13	Exod. 39–40	Prov. 18
Day 60	Matt. 8:14–34	Lev. 1–2	Prov. 19
Day 61	Matt. 9:1–17	Lev. 3–4	Prov. 20
Day 62	Matt. 9:18–38	Lev. 5–6	Prov. 21
Day 63	Matt. 10:1–25	Lev. 7–8	Prov. 22
Day 64	Matt. 10:26–42	Lev. 9–10	Prov. 23
Day 65	Matt. 11:1–19	Lev. 11–12	Prov. 24
Day 66	Matt. 11:20–30	Lev. 13	Prov. 25
Day 67	Matt. 12:1–21	Lev. 14	Prov. 26
Day 68	Matt. 12:22–50	Lev. 15–16	Prov. 27
Day 69	Matt. 13:1–23	Lev. 17–18	Prov. 28
Day 70	Matt. 13:24–58	Lev. 19	Prov. 29
Day 71	Matt. 14:1–21	Lev. 20–21	Prov. 30
Day 72	Matt. 14:22–36	Lev. 22–23	Prov. 31
Day 73	Matt. 15:1–20	Lev. 24–25	Eccles. 1:1–11
Day 74	Matt. 15:21–39	Lev. 26–27	Eccles. 1:12–2:26
Day 75	Matt. 16	Num. 1–2	Eccles. 3:1–15
Day 76	Matt. 17	Num. 3–4	Eccles. 3:16–4:16
Day 77	Matt. 18:1–20	Num. 5–6	Eccles. 5
Day 78	Matt. 18:21–35	Num. 7–8	Eccles. 6
Day 79	Matt. 19:1–15	Num. 9–10	Eccles. 7
Day 80	Matt. 19:16–30	Num. 11–12	Eccles. 8
Day 81	Matt. 20:1–16	Num. 13–14	Eccles. 9:1–12
Day 82	Matt. 20:17–34	Num. 15–16	Eccles. 9:13–10:20
Day 83	Matt. 21:1–27	Num. 17–18	Eccles. 11:1–8
Day 84	Matt. 21:28–46	Num. 19–20	Eccles. 11:9–12:14
Day 85	Matt. 22:1–22	Num. 21	Song of Sol. 1:1–2:7
Day 86	Matt. 22:23–46	Num. 22:1–40	Song of Sol. 2:8–3:5

Day 87	Matt. 23:1–12	Num. 22:41–23:26	Song of Sol. 3:6–5:1
Day 88	Matt. 23:13–39	Num. 23:27–24:25	Song of Sol. 5:2–6:3
Day 89	Matt. 24:1–31	Num. 25–27	Song of Sol. 6:4–8:4
Day 90	Matt. 24:32–51	Num. 28–29	Song of Sol. 8:5–14
Day 91	Matt. 25:1–30	Num. 30–31	Job 1
Day 92	Matt. 25:31–46	Num. 32–34	Job 2
Day 93	Matt. 26:1–25	Num. 35–36	Job 3
Day 94	Matt. 26:26–46	Deut. 1–2	Job 4
Day 95	Matt. 26:47–75	Deut. 3–4	Job 5
Day 96	Matt. 27:1–31	Deut. 5–6	Job 6
Day 97	Matt. 27:32–66	Deut. 7–8	Job 7
Day 98	Matt. 28	Deut. 9–10	Job 8
Day 99	Acts 1	Deut. 11–12	Job 9
Day 100	Acts 2:1–13	Deut. 13–14	Job 10
Day 101	Acts 2:14–47	Deut. 15–16	Job 11
Day 102	Acts 3	Deut. 17–18	Job 12
Day 103	Acts 4:1–22	Deut. 19–20	Job 13
Day 104	Acts 4:23–37	Deut. 21–22	Job 14
Day 105	Acts 5:1–16	Deut. 23–24	Job 15
Day 106	Acts 5:17–42	Deut. 25–27	Job 16
Day 107	Acts 6	Deut. 28	Job 17
Day 108	Acts 7:1–36	Deut. 29–30	Job 18
Day 109	Acts 7:37–60	Deut. 31–32	Job 19
Day 110	Acts 8:1–25	Deut. 33–34	Job 20
Day 111	Acts 8:26–40	Josh. 1–2	Job 21
Day 112	Acts 9:1–25	Josh. 3:1–5:1	Job 22
Day 113	Acts 9:26–43	Josh. 5:2–6:27	Job 23
Day 114	Acts 10:1–33	Josh. 7–8	Job 24
Day 115	Acts 10:34–48	Josh. 9–10	Job 25
Day 116	Acts 11:1–18	Josh. 11–12	Job 26
Day 117	Acts 11:19–30	Josh. 13–14	Job 27
Day 118	Acts 12	Josh. 15–17	Job 28

Day 119	Acts 13:1–25	Josh. 18–19	Job 29
Day 120	Acts 13:26–52	Josh. 20–21	Job 30
Day 121	Acts 14	Josh. 22	Job 31
Day 122	Acts 15:1–21	Josh. 23-24	Job 32
Day 123	Acts. 15:22–41	Judg. 1	Job 33
Day 124	Acts 16:1–15	Judg. 2–3	Job 34
Day 125	Acts 16:16–40	Judg. 4–5	Job 35
Day 126	Acts 17:1–15	Judg. 6	Job 36
Day 127	Acts 17:16–34	Judg. 7–8	Job 37
Day 128	Acts 18	Judg. 9	Job 38
Day 129	Acts 19:1–20	Judg. 10:1–11:33	Job 39
Day 130	Acts 19:21–41	Judg. 11:34–12:15	Job 40
Day 131	Acts 20:1–16	Judg. 13	Job 41
Day 132	Acts 20:17–38	Judg. 14–15	Job 42
Day 133	Acts 21:1–36	Judg. 16	Ps. 42
Day 134	Acts 21:37–22:29	Judg. 17–18	Ps. 43
Day 135	Acts 22:30–23:22	Judg. 19	Ps. 44
Day 136	Acts 23:23–24:9	Judg. 20	Ps. 45
Day 137	Acts 24:10–27	Judg. 21	Ps. 46
Day 138	Acts 25	Ruth 1–2	Ps. 47
Day 139	Acts 26:1–18	Ruth 3–4	Ps. 48
Day 140	Acts 26:19–32	1 Sam. 1:1–2:10	Ps. 49
Day 141	Acts 27:1–12	1 Sam. 2:11–36	Ps. 50
Day 142	Acts 27:13–44	1 Sam. 3	Ps. 51
Day 143	Acts 28:1–16	1 Sam. 4–5	Ps. 52
Day 144	Acts 28:17–31	1 Sam. 6–7	Ps. 53
Day 145	Rom. 1:1–15	1 Sam. 8	Ps. 54
Day 146	Rom. 1:16–32	1 Sam. 9:1–10:16	Ps. 55
Day 147	Rom. 2:1–3:8	1 Sam. 10:17–11:15	Ps. 56
Day 148	Rom. 3:9–31	1 Sam. 12	Ps. 57
Day 149	Rom. 4	1 Sam. 13	Ps. 58
Day 150	Rom. 5	1 Sam. 14	Ps. 59

Day 151	Rom. 6	1 Sam. 15	Ps. 60
Day 152	Rom. 7	1 Sam. 16	Ps. 61
Day 153	Rom. 8	1 Sam. 17:1–54	Ps. 62
Day 154	Rom. 9:1–29	1 Sam. 17:55–18:30	Ps. 63
Day 155	Rom. 9:30–10:21	1 Sam. 19	Ps. 64
Day 156	Rom. 11:1–24	1 Sam. 20	Ps. 65
Day 157	Rom. 11:25–36	1 Sam. 21–22	Ps. 66
Day 158	Rom. 12	1 Sam. 23–24	Ps. 67
Day 159	Rom. 13	1 Sam. 25	Ps. 68
Day 160	Rom. 14	1 Sam. 26	Ps. 69
Day 161	Rom. 15:1–13	1 Sam. 27–28	Ps. 70
Day 162	Rom. 15:14–33	1 Sam. 29–31	Ps. 71
Day 163	Rom. 16	2 Sam. 1	Ps. 72
Day 164	Mark 1:1–20	2 Sam. 2:1–3:1	Dan. 1
Day 165	Mark 1:21–45	2 Sam. 3:2–39	Dan. 2:1–23
Day 166	Mark 2	2 Sam. 4–5	Dan. 2:24–49
Day 167	Mark 3:1–19	2 Sam. 6	Dan. 3
Day 168	Mark 3:20–35	2 Sam. 7–8	Dan. 4
Day 169	Mark 4:1–20	2 Sam. 9–10	Dan. 5
Day 170	Mark 4:21–41	2 Sam. 11–12	Dan. 6
Day 171	Mark 5:1–20	2 Sam. 13	Dan. 7
Day 172	Mark 5:21–43	2 Sam. 14	Dan. 8
Day 173	Mark 6:1–29	2 Sam. 15	Dan. 9
Day 174	Mark 6:30–56	2 Sam. 16	Dan. 10:1–21
Day 175	Mark 7:1–13	2 Sam. 17	Dan. 11:1–19
Day 176	Mark 7:14–37	2 Sam. 18	Dan. 11:20–45
Day 177	Mark 8:1–21	2 Sam. 19	Dan. 12
Day 178	Mark 8:22–9:1	2 Sam. 20–21	Hosea 1:1–2:1
Day 179	Mark 9:2–50	2 Sam. 22	Hosea 2:2–23
Day 180	Mark 10:1–31	2 Sam. 23	Hosea 3
Day 181	Mark 10:32–52	2 Sam. 24	Hosea 4:1–11
Day 182	Mark 11:1–14	1 Kings 1	Hosea 4:12–5:4

Day 183	Mark 11:15–33	1 Kings 2	Hosea 5:5–15
Day 184	Mark 12:1–27	1 Kings 3	Hosea 6:1–7:2
Day 185	Mark 12:28–44	1 Kings 4–5	Hosea 7:3–16
Day 186	Mark 13:1–13	1 Kings 6	Hosea 8
Day 187	Mark 13:14–37	1 Kings 7	Hosea 9:1–16
Day 188	Mark 14:1–31	1 Kings 8	Hosea 9:17–10:15
Day 189	Mark 14:32–72	1 Kings 9	Hosea 11:1–11
Day 190	Mark 15:1–20	1 Kings 10	Hosea 11:12–12:14
Day 191	Mark 15:21–47	1 Kings 11	Hosea 13
Day 192	Mark 16	1 Kings 12:1–31	Hosea 14
Day 193	1 Cor. 1:1–17	1 Kings 12:32–13:34	Joel 1
Day 194	1 Cor. 1:18–31	1 Kings 14	Joel 2:1–11
Day 195	1 Cor. 2	1 Kings 15:1–32	Joel 2:12–32
Day 196	1 Cor. 3	1 Kings 15:33–16:34	Joel 3
Day 197	1 Cor. 4	1 Kings 17	Amos 1
Day 198	1 Cor. 5	1 Kings 18	Amos 2:1–3:2
Day 199	1 Cor. 6	1 Kings 19	Amos 3:3–4:3
Day 200	1 Cor. 7:1–24	1 Kings 20	Amos 4:4–13
Day 201	1 Cor. 7:25–40	1 Kings 21	Amos 5
Day 202	1 Cor. 8	1 Kings 22	Amos 6
Day 203	1 Cor. 9	2 Kings 1–2	Amos 7
Day 204	1 Cor. 10	2 Kings 3	Amos 8
Day 205	1 Cor. 11:1–16	2 Kings 4	Amos 9
Day 206	1 Cor. 11:17–34	2 Kings 5	Obadiah 1
Day 207	1 Cor. 12	2 Kings 6:1–7:2	Jonah 1
Day 208	1 Cor. 13	2 Kings 7:3–20	Jonah 2
Day 209	1 Cor. 14:1–25	2 Kings 8	Jonah 3
Day 210	1 Cor. 14:26–40	2 Kings 9	Jonah 4
Day 211	1 Cor. 15:1–34	2 Kings 10	Mic. 1
Day 212	1 Cor. 15:35–58	2 Kings 11	Mic. 2
Day 213	1 Cor. 16	2 Kings 12–13	Mic. 3
Day 214	2 Cor. 1:1–2:4	2 Kings 14	Mic. 4:1–5:1

Day 215	2 Cor. 2:5–3:18	2 Kings 15–16	Mic. 5:2–15
Day 216	2 Cor. 4:1–5:10	2 Kings 17	Mic. 6
Day 217	2 Cor. 5:11–6:13	2 Kings 18	Mic. 7
Day 218	2 Cor. 6:14–7:16	2 Kings 19	Nah. 1
Day 219	2 Cor. 8	2 Kings 20–21	Nah. 2
Day 220	2 Cor. 9	2 Kings 22:1–23:35	Nah. 3
Day 221	2 Cor. 10	2 Kings 23:36–24:20	Hab. 1
Day 222	2 Cor. 11	2 Kings 25	Hab. 2
Day 223	2 Cor. 12	1 Chron. 1–2	Hab. 3
Day 224	2 Cor. 13	1 Chron. 3–4	Zeph. 1
Day 225	John 1:1–18	1 Chron. 5–6	Zeph. 2
Day 226	John 1:19–34	1 Chron. 7–8	Zeph. 3
Day 227	John 1:35–51	1 Chron. 9	Hag. 1–2
Day 228	John 2	1 Chron. 10–11	Zech. 1
Day 229	John 3:1–21	1 Chron. 12	Zech. 2
Day 230	John 3:22–36	1 Chron. 13–14	Zech. 3
Day 231	John 4:1–26	1 Chron. 15:1–16:6	Zech. 4
Day 232	John 4:27–42	1 Chron. 16:7–43	Zech. 5
Day 233	John 4:43–54	1 Chron. 17	Zech. 6
Day 234	John 5:1–18	1 Chron. 18–19	Zech. 7
Day 235	John 5:19–47	1 Chron. 20:1–22:1	Zech. 8
Day 236	John 6:1–21	1 Chron. 22:2–23:32	Zech. 9
Day 237	John 6:22–59	1 Chron. 24	Zech. 10
Day 238	John 6:60–71	1 Chron. 25–26	Zech. 11
Day 239	John 7:1–24	1 Chron. 27–28	Zech. 12
Day 240	John 7:25–52	1 Chron. 29	Zech. 13
Day 241	John 8:1–20	2 Chron. 1:1–2:16	Zech. 14
Day 242	John 8:21–47	2 Chron. 2:17–5:1	Mal. 1:1–2:9
Day 243	John 8:48–59	2 Chron. 5:2–14	Mal. 2:10–16
Day 244	John 9:1–23	2 Chron. 6	Mal. 2:17–3:18
Day 245	John 9:24–41	2 Chron. 7	Mal. 4
Day 246	John 10:1–21	2 Chron. 8	Ps. 73

Day 247	John 10:22–42	2 Chron. 9	Ps. 74
Day 248	John 11:1–27	2 Chron. 10–11	Ps. 75
Day 249	John 11:28–57	2 Chron. 12–13	Ps. 76
Day 250	John 12:1–26	2 Chron. 14–15	Ps. 77
Day 251	John 12:27–50	2 Chron. 16–17	Ps. 78:1–20
Day 252	John 13:1–20	2 Chron. 18	Ps. 78:21–37
Day 253	John 13:21–38	2 Chron. 19	Ps. 78:38–55
Day 254	John 14:1–14	2 Chron. 20:1–21:1	Ps. 78:56–72
Day 255	John 14:15–31	2 Chron. 21:2–22:12	Ps. 79
Day 256	John 15:1–16:4	2 Chron. 23	Ps. 80
Day 257	John 16:5–33	2 Chron. 24	Ps. 81
Day 258	John 17	2 Chron. 25	Ps. 82
Day 259	John 18:1–18	2 Chron. 26	Ps. 83
Day 260	John 18:19–38	2 Chron. 27–28	Ps. 84
Day 261	John 18:39–19:16	2 Chron. 29	Ps. 85
Day 262	John 19:17–42	2 Chron. 30	Ps. 86
Day 263	John 20:1–18	2 Chron. 31	Ps. 87
Day 264	John 20:19–31	2 Chron. 32	Ps. 88
Day 265	John 21	2 Chron. 33	Ps. 89:1–18
Day 266	1 John 1	2 Chron. 34	Ps. 89:19–37
Day 267	1 John 2	2 Chron. 35	Ps. 89:38–52
Day 268	1 John 3	2 Chron. 36	Ps. 90
Day 269	1 John 4	Ezra 1–2	Ps. 91
Day 270	1 John 5	Ezra 3–4	Ps. 92
Day 271	2 John	Ezra 5–6	Ps. 93
Day 272	3 John	Ezra 7–8	Ps. 94
Day 273	Jude	Ezra 9–10	Ps. 95
Day 274	Rev. 1	Neh. 1–2	Ps. 96
Day 275	Rev. 2	Neh. 3	Ps. 97
Day 276	Rev. 3	Neh. 4	Ps. 98
Day 277	Rev. 4	Neh. 5:1–7:4	Ps. 99
Day 278	Rev. 5	Neh. 7:5–8:12	Ps. 100

Day 279	Rev. 6	Neh. 8:13–9:37	Ps. 101
Day 280	Rev. 7	Neh. 9:38–10:39	Ps. 102
Day 281	Rev. 8	Neh. 11	Ps. 103
Day 282	Rev. 9	Neh. 12	Ps. 104:1–23
Day 283	Rev. 10	Neh. 13	Ps. 104:24–35
Day 284	Rev. 11	Esther 1	Ps. 105:1–25
Day 285	Rev. 12	Esther 2	Ps. 105:26–45
Day 286	Rev. 13	Esther 3–4	Ps. 106:1–23
Day 287	Rev. 14	Esther 5:1–6:13	Ps. 106:24–48
Day 288	Rev. 15	Esther 6:14–8:17	Ps. 107:1–22
Day 289	Rev. 16	Esther 9–10	Ps. 107:23–43
Day 290	Rev. 17	Isa. 1–2	Ps. 108
Day 291	Rev. 18	Isa. 3–4	Ps. 109:1–19
Day 292	Rev. 19	Isa. 5–6	Ps. 109:20–31
Day 293	Rev. 20	Isa. 7–8	Ps. 110
Day 294	Rev. 21–22	Isa. 9–10	Ps. 111
Day 295	1 Thess. 1	Isa. 11–13	Ps. 112
Day 296	1 Thess. 2:1–16	Isa. 14–16	Ps. 113
Day 297	1 Thess. 2:17–3:13	Isa. 17–19	Ps. 114
Day 298	1 Thess. 4	Isa. 20–22	Ps. 115
Day 299	1 Thess. 5	Isa. 23–24	Ps. 116
Day 300	2 Thess. 1	Isa. 25–26	Ps. 117
Day 301	2 Thess. 2	Isa. 27–28	Ps. 118
Day 302	2 Thess. 3	Isa. 29–30	Ps. 119:1–32
Day 303	1 Tim. 1	Isa. 31–33	Ps. 119:33–64
Day 304	1 Tim. 2	Isa. 34–35	Ps. 119:65–96
Day 305	1 Tim. 3	Isa. 36–37	Ps. 119:97–120
Day 306	1 Tim. 4	Isa. 38–39	Ps. 119:121–144
Day 307	1 Tim. 5:1–22	Jer. 1–2	Ps. 119:145–176
Day 308	1 Tim. 5:23–6:21	Jer. 3–4	Ps. 120
Day 309	2 Tim. 1	Jer. 5–6	Ps. 121
Day 310	2 Tim. 2	Jer. 7–8	Ps. 122

Day 311	2 Tim. 3	Jer. 9–10	Ps. 123
Day 312	2 Tim. 4	Jer. 11-12	Ps. 124
Day 313	Titus 1	Jer. 13–14	Ps. 125
Day 314	Titus 2	Jer. 15–16	Ps. 126
Day 315	Titus 3	Jer. 17–18	Ps. 127
Day 316	Philemon	Jer. 19–20	Ps. 128
Day 317	James 1	Jer. 21–22	Ps. 129
Day 318	James 2	Jer. 23–24	Ps. 130
Day 319	James 3	Jer. 25–26	Ps. 131
Day 320	James 4	Jer. 27–28	Ps. 132
Day 321	James 5	Jer. 29–30	Ps. 133
Day 322	1 Pet. 1	Jer. 31–32	Ps. 134
Day 323	1 Pet. 2	Jer. 33–34	Ps. 135
Day 324	1 Pet. 3	Jer. 35–36	Ps. 136
Day 325	1 Pet. 4	Jer. 37–38	Ps. 137
Day 326	1 Pet. 5	Jer. 39–40	Ps. 138
Day 327	2 Pet. 1	Jer. 41–42	Ps. 139
Day 328	2 Pet. 2	Jer. 43–44	Ps. 140
Day 329	2 Pet. 3	Jer. 45–46	Ps. 141
Day 330	Gal. 1	Jer. 47–48	Ps. 142
Day 331	Gal. 2	Jer. 49–50	Ps. 143
Day 332	Gal. 3:1–18	Jer. 51–52	Ps. 144
Day 333	Gal. 3:19–4:20	Lam. 1–2	Ps. 145
Day 334	Gal. 4:21–31	Lam. 3–4	Ps. 146
Day 335	Gal. 5:1–15	Lam. 5	Ps. 147
Day 336	Gal. 5:16–26	Ezek. 1	Ps. 148
Day 337	Gal. 6	Ezek. 2–3	Ps. 149
Day 338	Eph. 1	Ezek. 4–5	Ps. 150
Day 339	Eph. 2	Ezek. 6–7	Isa. 40
Day 340	Eph. 3	Ezek. 8–9	Isa. 41
Day 341	Eph. 4:1–16	Ezek. 10–11	Isa. 42
Day 342	Eph. 4:17–32	Ezek. 12–13	Isa. 43

Day 343	Eph. 5:1–20	Ezek. 14–15	Isa. 44
Day 344	Eph. 5:21–33	Ezek. 16	Isa. 45
Day 345	Eph. 6	Ezek. 17	Isa. 46
Day 346	Phil. 1:1–11	Ezek. 18	Isa. 47
Day 347	Phil. 1:12–30	Ezek. 19	Isa. 48
Day 348	Phil 2:1–11	Ezek. 20	Isa. 49
Day 349	Phil. 2:12–30	Ezek. 21–22	Isa. 50
Day 350	Phil. 3	Ezek. 23	Isa. 51
Day 351	Phil. 4	Ezek. 24	Isa. 52
Day 352	Col. 1:1–23	Ezek. 25–26	Isa. 53
Day 353	Col. 1:24–2:19	Ezek. 27–28	Isa. 54
Day 354	Col. 2:20–3:17	Ezek. 29–30	Isa. 55
Day 355	Col. 3:18–4:18	Ezek. 31–32	Isa. 56
Day 356	Luke 1:1–25	Ezek. 33	Isa. 57
Day 357	Luke 1:26–56	Ezek. 34	Isa. 58
Day 358	Luke 1:57–80	Ezek. 35–36	Isa. 59
Day 359	Luke 2:1–20	Ezek. 37	Isa. 60
Day 360	Luke 2:21–52	Ezek. 38–39	Isa. 61
Day 361	Luke 3:1–20	Ezek. 40–41	Isa. 62
Day 362	Luke 3:21–38	Ezek. 42–43	Isa. 63
Day 363	Luke 4:1–30	Ezek. 44–45	Isa. 64
Day 364	Luke 4:31–44	Ezek. 46–47	Isa. 65
Day 365	Luke 5:1–26	Ezek. 48	Isa. 66

Spiritual Birth Certificate

for

_____
(name)

_____
(date)

"Whoever calls on the name of the Lord shall be saved." Romans 10:13

Knowing that I have sinned and that I need the Lord Jesus Christ as my Savior, I now turn from my sins and trust Him for my eternal life. I ask Jesus Christ to forgive me, to deliver me from sin's power, and to give me eternal life. I now give Jesus Christ control of my life. From this time forward, as He gives me strength, I will seek to trust and obey Him in all areas of my life.

_____
Pastor/Leader Signature

About the Author

Jimmy Evans is a long-time pastor, Bible teacher, and best-selling author. He is the Founder and President of XO Marriage, a ministry devoted to helping couples thrive in strong and fulfilling marriages.

For 30 years, Jimmy ministered as Senior Pastor of Trinity Fellowship Church in Amarillo, Texas, where he now serves as Apostolic Elder. During his time as senior pastor the church grew from 900 to over 10,000 members. Jimmy loves mentoring pastors and helping local churches grow to reach their potential. He is a popular speaker at churches and leadership conferences across America.

Jimmy has written more than 18 books, including *Marriage on the Rock*, *The Four Laws of Love*, *21 Day Inner Healing*, *Tipping Point*, and *Where Are the Missing People*.

Jimmy and Karen have been married for 49 years and have two married children and five grandchildren.

Marriage Help

We understand that when your marriage is struggling, you need help in a timely manner. XO Marriage is here to support you and stand alongside you in the fight for your marriage. We offer two distinct services:

Coaching on Call

Offered at multiple lengths, these sessions are designed for couples or individuals who are in crisis and need immediate help. Specializing in marital crisis intervention, our team is available to meet you in your time of need to listen with compassion and understanding, provide wise objective counsel, and help you navigate the best plan of action to start the healing process.

Marriage Mediation

Our full day private one-on-one marriage mediation is designed for couples who are struggling with multiple issues and/or feeling hopeless about the future of their marriage. This intensive approach allows couples the extended time needed to fully process their primary issues without the interruption of time or hassle of scheduling multiple weekly sessions.

To learn more, visit **xomarriage.com/help**.